The Iphigenia Plays

NORTHWESTERN WORLD CLASSICS

*Northwestern World Classics brings readers
the world's greatest literature. The series features
essential new editions of well-known works,
lesser-known books that merit reconsideration,
and lost classics of fiction, drama, and poetry.
Insightful commentary and compelling new translations
help readers discover the joy of outstanding writing
from all regions of the world.*

Euripides

The Iphigenia Plays
New Verse Translations

Translated from the Greek by Rachel Hadas

Northwestern University Press ✦ *Evanston, Illinois*

Northwestern University Press
www.nupress.northwestern.edu

Printed in the United States of America

10   9   8   7   6   5   4   3   2   1

ISBN 978-0-8101-3723-3 (paper)
ISBN 978-0-8101-3724-0 (ebook)

Library of Congress Cataloging-in-Publication Data

Names: Euripides, author. | Hadas, Rachel. translator. | Euripides.
    Iphigenia in Aulis. English. (Hadas) | Euripides. Iphigenia in Tauris.
    English. (Hadas)
Title: Euripides : the Iphigenia plays : new verse translations / Euripides ;
    translated from the Greek by Rachel Hadas.
Other titles: Iphigenia plays
Description: Evanston, Illinois : Northwestern University Press, 2018.
Identifiers: LCCN 2017058652 | ISBN 9780810137233 (pbk. : alk. paper) |
    ISBN 9780810137240 (ebook)
Classification: LCC PA3975.A2 2018 | DDC 882.01—dc23
LC record available at https://lccn.loc.gov/2017058652

These translations are in memory of my parents,
classicists and lovers of learning
who passed their passion on to me:

Moses Hadas, 1900–1966
Elizabeth Chamberlayne Hadas, 1915–1992

CONTENTS

Stories about Iphigenia weren't new when Euripides wrote his plays about her. To take only the most familiar examples of treatments with which Euripides certainly would have been familiar, the chorus of Aeschylus' *Agamemnon* (458 B.C.E.) evokes, without precisely describing it, the sacrifice of the girl. A century or more earlier than the Aeschylean play, Homer, drawing on generations of oral poetry, omitted any reference to Iphigenia in *The Iliad*. The only exception to the Iliadic silence on this subject occurs in book 9, the so-called embassy scene. In the hope that Achilles will emerge from sulking in his tent and help the Greek army, Agamemnon offers the recalcitrant hero any one of his three daughters in marriage. The daughters are named Electra, Chrysothemis, and Iphianassa. The offer is contemptuously rebuffed; plenty of girls back home, says Achilles, would love to marry me. Still, the fictive marriage between Achilles and Iphigenia is a sturdy ghost, which surfaces in Euripides' plays as well as in many subsequent treatments of the story. Racine's 1674 tragedy *Iphigénie en Aulide*, Goethe's *Iphigenia in Tauris* (1779–86), and Barry Unsworth's 2003 novel *The Songs of the Kings* are three masterful and very different revisitings of the tale across the centuries. In addition, a prolific crop of plays and libretti by writers now mostly forgotten appeared throughout the eighteenth century. Michalis Cacoyannis' 1978 film *Iphigenia* draws heavily on Euripides' *Iphigenia in Aulis*. And then there are the shorter versions, such as Lucretius' lapidary retelling of the story of the sacrifice to make the point that *tantum religio potuit suadere malorum*.[1] H.D., in her long modernist poem *Helen in Egypt* (1960), devotes a fair amount of space to Iphigenia. Closer to us in time are the dramas of Charles Mee. And more Iphigenias will undoubtedly keep cropping up; a recent example is Colm Toibin's 2017 novel *House of Names*.

Yet no matter how numerous and how familiar stories around Iphigenia were and are, these tales always sustain—and, more than sustain, demand—a lot of retelling. No matter the version, there is always something elliptical, incomplete, and puzzling about the story; no one ever sees the whole picture. This is certainly true of the Euripidean plays about Iphigenia, even though both offer us plenty of information. The condition of the text of *Iphigenia in Aulis* makes it hard to know exactly where that play begins; but sometime early in the action, Agamemnon runs through the history that has led up to his present dilemma for the benefit of the Old Man—and of the audience. And *Iphigenia in Tauris* opens with the familiar Euripidean prologue, in which a character fills us in on who and where they are and what the situation is.

As both these plays unfold, the characters continue to go over and over the events of the past—a feature of Euripides' treatment of myth that has been best captured by Yannis Ritsos' remarkable dramatic monologues in his 1972 collection *The Fourth Dimension.* It's striking how little these recitals suffer from staleness. For one thing, the reiterations occur in different contexts and different emotional keys, now explanatory, now accusatory, now matter-of-fact, now emotional. Then, too, Ritsos adds anachronistic touches like a tourist bus or a cigarette.

Sometimes the recitation of past events is an effort to make sense of the present—how did we get exactly here? Sometimes it's a correction of some misconception, or part of an argument that, as often in Euripides, would fit smoothly into a courtroom drama. Often there's the sense of a trauma retold, not so much to air old grievances as simply to bring horror to light—to give nightmarish events, or even events that really were dreams, meaning by casting them into language.

I read *Iphigenia in Aulis* as a tragedy, a play that gathers momentum as it marches inexorably toward a terrible ending. Accordingly, language in this play can clarify but cannot help or cure. Perhaps in the swirl and momentum of events this play portrays, language cannot even persuade; critics have been uncertain how to take Iphigenia's change of heart from terror to resignation to heroism. A mocking, ghostly irony hovers over the situation and infects or inflects the language, and yet I find it hard to read this play as simply ironic. Listening to Iphigenia's words, I find them moving partly because they somehow ring true. *Iphigenia in Tauris*, on the other hand, is a romance, which features a hairsbreadth escape and a triumphant ending. In this play, accordingly, language throws light on the murky passages of the past, facilitates recognition and childhood memories, strengthens family ties, and solves seemingly intractable problems.

In both plays, Euripides' command of suspenseful plotting is matched by his superb psychological insights. At the start of *Iphigenia in Tauris*, the heroine narrates and then promptly interprets the dream she has just had about her brother: "My dream brought strange visions last night;/let me tell them to the morning light,/if that can help." I was reminded of an anecdote told by James Merrill in a 1975 essay about Cavafy: "I have heard a mother advise her child to tell its bad dream to the lighted bulb hanging from a kitchen ceiling."[2] These repeated visitings of past horrors, whether the horrors endured were experienced or only dreamed, also put me in mind of the description of Freud's technique in W. H. Auden's elegy "In Memory of Sigmund Freud":[3]

> He wasn't clever at all: he merely told
> The unhappy Present to recite the Past
> Like a poetry lesson till sooner
> Or later it faltered at the line where
>
> Long ago the accusations had begun,
> And suddenly knew by whom it had been judged . . .

The long, exhausted, and exhaustive monologues in Yannis Ritsos' *The Fourth Dimension*, a too little known book which I've already mentioned, also exemplify their speakers' insatiable need to understand and relieve the traumas of the past by repeated telling and retelling. In the case of Ritsos' poems, the hapless listener (not to mention the reader) is something like the hapless wedding guest in *The Ancient Mariner*, buttonholed into hearing a complicated history. In Euripides' plays, by contrast, the listener is (or so I imagine) breathless with interest.

Sooner or later, though, the characters in these plays stop dwelling on the past. Euripides is well known to be an expert in pathology, but he is also a master of vivid depictions of brisk, no-nonsense characters (especially women) with great executive ability. In *Iphigenia in Aulis*, the youthful heroine, once she has made up her mind to die, calmly issues orders (don't cut your hair; don't wear black) to her distraught mother. In the Taurian sequel, Iphigenia is a quintessential elder sister, used to taking command of any situation; she has a much better head for planning than her wayward younger brother does. (In this respect, Iphigenia is to Orestes rather as Helen, in the eponymous Euripidean romance, is to the ineffective Menelaus.) Iphigenia is a survivor who can calmly refer to her own death. Perhaps this sangfroid is contagious. For whatever reason, at a certain point in the Taurian play, both Iphigenia and Orestes seem able to leave the many horrors of their family history behind. When Athena comes down from the machine to issue orders and ensure the Greeks' escape at the drama's close, the goddess seems like the elder sister Iphigenia's own elder sister—larger than life but recognizable.

One of the many pleasures of spending more than three years with these plays was my growing confidence in what I would find as I worked. I knew that I would encounter such well-known dramatic features as pace—the way Euripides intersperses fraught dialogue with lyric interludes and moments of suspense. I expected surges of emotion in the choruses. But I also came to count on the striking realism of the characterizations. It's a commonplace that Euripides, unlike his fellow tragedians, shows people not as they should be but as they are. His people are recognizable in extreme situations which seem perfectly plausible because of the human dynamics that we see played out. Agamemnon's quarrel with Menelaus in *Iphigenia in Aulis* is an outstanding example (Cacoyannis hardly needed to change a word of Euripides' dialogue for his film); but both the Iphigenia plays furnish other examples. Also in *Aulis*, Agamemnon's exchanges with Clytemnestra contrast comically with the queen's conversations with Achilles, whom she at first assumes is her future son-in-law. In both plays, there's plenty of wry situational and even verbal irony based on misunderstandings and subterfuges. But, as befits a play which is less a tragedy than a romance, the misunderstandings, recognitions, and double takes in *Iphigenia in Tauris* are essentially comic. Time in this play is on everyone's side—what was thought lost is recovered—whereas in *Iphigenia in Aulis*, time is on no one's side. The confusion in Aulis gives way to a clarity that is bitter and dreadful.

Not that Euripides is purely or simply a realist. His psychological verisimilitude plays out against an oneiric backdrop. *Iphigenia in Aulis* resembles a nightmare from which a whole family is unable to wake up. The dreamy quality is both more benign and more pronounced in the Taurian play, as befits a drama that begins with the telling of a dream. Was Iphigenia's rescue to Taurus all a dream? What about Orestes' long flight? The statue unaccountably falling from heaven?

No sooner has the Taurian play begun than Iphigenia confides to us her dream; and it's characteristic of her that she is sure what it means. Her own situation, however outlandish, is stable; she knows her status and her role, and indeed she sometimes seems reasonably comfortable with them, until the time comes for family loyalty to trump sacrificial ritual. Blood, we might say, is thicker than blood. Orestes, with his hallucinations and his apparent epileptic fits, has his own nightmare aura. But note how realistically his personality is drawn. Even when he isn't hallucinating, he's skittish, fearful, prone to sudden bad ideas (Desert this place, turn around and go home! No, kill the king!) which are tactfully quashed by the calmer people around him. (Carolyn Kizer observes that Pylades and Thoas are two of the saner characters in this play.)[4] Our last glimpse of Orestes, with his sister on his shoulder and clutching the all-important statue of Artemis in his opposite hand, is at once heroic (he's carrying the burden, he's escaping) and poignant (he's weighed down by the very female forces that succor him). They have supported him; now he is (literally) supporting them. Kizer isn't wrong to observe that "in regarding these characters [Iphigenia and Orestes] it is perhaps best to think of them as partly crazy." And yet at the same time, the sister and brother are sane enough, at least in this play, to survive, escape, and carry on.

Beyond subtleties of characterization, beyond Euripides' ability to endow a mythical plot with convincing realism, the feature that repeatedly struck me was the remarkable resilience of these characters—a resilience which again feels very true to life. As soon as one crisis is past, the survivors must decide, and decide immediately, what to do next. It helps if someone is in charge. Like Helen in her eponymous Euripidean play, Iphigenia in *Iphigenia in Tauris*, from having been a virtual prisoner in a foreign country, effortlessly takes command. She is remarkably good at foreseeing complications and lying when necessary—lying with an Odyssean panache. The joy and excitement that infuse this drama have as much to do with the sense of recovered agency, with the play of intelligence and ingenuity, as they do with the moving family reunions. If the passage in which sister and brother celebrate their mutual recognition and recovery is operatic, the step-by-step plotting that follows, half planned and half improvised, is both suspenseful and comic. Again, a Homeric note is struck. There's a time for tears, as Telemachus reminds his hosts Helen and Menelaus in book 4 of *The Odyssey*, but we also need to sleep and eat. And in the case of Iphigenia, Orestes, and Pylades, we need to plot our escape. Past horrors are past. Again, like *The Odyssey*, this play is a postwar piece about the challenges of survival and the need to carry on.

And there's more. Euripides' characters, I saw again and again, are not only beautifully observed themselves; they are also possessed of remarkable insights into human behavior. Some of these perceptions are familiar ones, well-worn truths. After all, we count on Greek choruses to tell us what we already know rather than to surprise us with fresh insights. This purveying of well-worn truths is part of what drama offers. When Agamemnon, at the start of *Iphigenia in Aulis*, tells the Old Man that he envies him his peaceful obscurity, his ability to sleep at night, the king's words bear a family resemblance to Henry V's nighttime soliloquy before the battle of Agincourt, which probably already sounded familiar to Shakespeare's audience. But other sayings, no less true to human nature, are a bit more unexpected, as when Iphigenia observes that once one has settled on a course of action, however risky, one can't help worrying about details: "People in trouble do not have a prayer/of calm once they have left behind despair/and turned toward hope." Or when she comments that people who have experienced misfortune all their lives are better equipped to deal with bad luck than fortunate people are:

The man who has never had good luck—
I envy him! When he is struck
by a change of fortune from good to bad,
he does not miss what he never had.
Accustomed to hard necessity,
he is inured to misery.
But to have tasted peace and joy,
and then to lose them, seems to me
a heavy fate for mortals to bear,
a burden of endless misery.

Iphigenia is also frank about resenting people whose lives are easier than hers: "We who have suffered a harsh fate/are not fond of the fortunate." Orestes has a moment of testy insight when he rejects Iphigenia's proffered sympathy at his impending sacrifice:

If you plan
to kill someone,
it makes no sense to try
to ease their dread of death with sympathy.

A moving example of the characters' insight into their own situations occurs when Iphigenia confesses that she hardly knows how to welcome the joy she feels at her reunion with her brother. Joy is strange to her:

This joy, this pleasure
is so new to me
I fear it will grow wings and fly
out of my hands into the sky.

This psychological realism, no matter how exotic the backdrop, extends to the chorus, particularly in the Taurian play. Granted, the chorus's generic inability to affect the action poses a dramatic challenge; Euripidean heroines regularly beg the chorus to keep a secret. But when the chorus and the heroine long for the same thing, as is the case here, the improbability fades. I used to find tragic choruses hard to swallow, but as I get older, I'm struck more by the verisimilitude of the situation: a group of well-meaning and articulate friends and neighbors, inevitably with troubles of their own, who are intensely sympathetic but can't do much to help. Only the other day I happened to read in a magazine's advice column about how to talk to bereaved people: "Don't be afraid of speaking in clichés. People aren't counting on you to provide the brilliant gem that will fix things. Your presence and your caring are what they appreciate." I doubt if Robert Zucker, writing in *Real Simple*, had Greek choruses in mind, but he might as well have.

In Euripides, as in Greek tragedy in general, the members of the chorus sometimes seem to be speaking or chanting in unison. At other times, as when the excited women in *Iphigenia in Aulis* describe their glimpses of Greek heroes, the members of the chorus are evidently speaking one at a time, their words almost tumbling over one another (as Cacoyannis interprets the scene in his film). The very ambiguity of the tradition leaves plenty of room for interpretive leeway; decisions about staging choral interludes are best left to directors. What's important to me is that choral utterances have a different pace and pulse from the dialogue portions of the plays: speedy, lyrical, intense. Yet it is also well known that the choral voice(s) can sometimes sound a cautious note, pragmatic and calm. And to complicate matters further, some of Iphigenia's most poignant utterances, which are often laments, are in choral metrics rather than the calmer iambics of the dialogue or of expository passages. For example, the passage in the Taurian play where Iphigenia mourns, "I am a stranger in my life" is in lyric, not iambic, meter.

When it comes to plot, *Iphigenia in Aulis* has an open ending— what I tell my students is a soft spot in the myth, a fogginess that extends beyond the problematic end of the play, when the doe is reportedly sacrificed on the altar in place of Iphigenia. What has happened to the young woman? Has she really been rescued and flown off with by Artemis to a new home by the Black Sea and an alarmingly resonant new career as a priestess of Artemis whose function is to sacrifice foreigners? *Iphigenia in Aulis*, if only because of the conveniently tattered condition of the text, leaves open more than one answer to that question. Racine's play *Iphigénie en Aulide* and Barry Unsworth's novel *The Songs of the Kings* provide very different answers. It is remarkable that so stark and catastrophic an ending—the ending we tend to believe in, the ending toward which the play seems to be moving—radiates out into so many ambiguous alternative possibilities, each compelling on its own terms.

Euripides' romance *Helen* similarly offers alternative versions of events. But the version of Helen's story the poet Stesichorus wrote—the version Euripides and, much later, H.D. spun out into their poetry—is, however unsettling, less radical a spin. However you read the story of Helen, whether or not you believe she went to Troy, the woman survives the war; and the play takes place after the war is over. The end of the story of Iphigenia, on the other hand, offers the alternatives of life or death. For the reader or hearer or beholder faced with this stark choice, the stakes seem higher. And if the plots are open-ended, the range of our possible responses is even more so. Horror; indignation; disbelief; relief; amusement: where on this spectrum does each of us find ourselves?

In the fall of 2016, I taught both the Iphigenia plays, in my father Moses Hadas' clear prose translation, to graduate students in a Rutgers seminar on myth and literature. I hadn't consciously planned for our readings about Iphigenia to occur in October and November, and so to coincide with the climax of the presidential campaign and with the election, but that's what happened. Unprompted, my students pounced with alarm and gusto on the parallels between the drama we were living through, on the one hand, and the sacrifice of Iphigenia, on the other.

Not for the first time, I found myself disagreeing with Walt Whitman's airy dismissal of classical mythology in his 1871 poem "Song of the Exposition":[5]

> Come Muse migrate from Greece and Ionia,
> Cross out please those immensely overpaid accounts,
> That matter of Troy and Achilles' wrath, and Aeneas', Odysseus'
> wanderings,
> Placard "Removed" and "To Let" on the rocks of your snowy
> Parnassus. . . .

Whitman calls for "a better, fresher, busier sphere, a wide, untried domain." But his breezy optimism, his airy dismissal of stale grievances, didn't seem to pertain to the world we found ourselves living in that fall. Instead, my students were mesmerized by the darkly compelling, ironic, and ambiguous story about the ambitious, ruthless father and the nubile daughter, the family whose struggle loomed larger than life. In the few weeks remaining to us after November 9, three of my dozen students—all women—chose for their final projects to write imaginative pieces based on, or spinning off, or adding to the Iphigenia story. Ariel wrote a short play about Trump's campaign and the use to which he puts Ivanka. Jodi wrote a dialogue in which two partners argue about the interpretation of *Iphigenia in Aulis*, which one them has just staged for a local theater. Sara wrote a sequence of poems presenting various points of view about the Iphigenia story.

None of these young women seemed to feel the impulse to cross out overpaid accounts or placard "Remove" on the rocks of Parnassus. Rather, they were exulting—almost wallowing—in the thickness, richness, and grisly relevance of the murky old story. All their work was strikingly multivocal; each retelling of the story seemed to demand a range of subjectivities, playing out differently for each person involved. Furthermore, each of these students ventured beyond her habitual mode to explore this tangled tale. Ariel, a poet, had never tried to write a play. Jodi, a fiction writer, was only beginning to discover dialogue. And Sara, an MA student who wasn't in the MFA program, was used to writing analytically about literature rather than writing poems. But the overpaid mythical accounts, it turned out, begged for more payment. The "better, fresher, busier sphere" might be something to aspire to later—but at the moment, it must have seemed underimagined and bland, compared to the rich brew these students found themselves working with.

To understand a myth, you almost have to retell it, and you inevitably change it in the retelling. Tim Mayo's poem "Taxonomies" captures the blank-check quality of a powerful yet ambiguous story open not only to retelling and to interpretation but to something more radical.[6] Mayo writes of

how myth changes: first, a deep
annunciating thump arrives in your ribcage,

then, you twist the smooth pages of the old story,
crumpling them up and flattening them out, scratching
their surface until the ink relinquishes its authority,
and the words tell it the way you've always felt

it should be.

"Crumpling them up and flattening them out": "Shall I uncrumple
this much-crumpled thing?" asks the speaker in Wallace Stevens'
"Le Monocle de Mon Oncle."[7] The creases, however, remain. Euripides uncrumpled an old story and added new creases. My students
crumpled and uncrumpled and recrumpled the story. The possibilities, the ramifications, seemed endless. There was no simple or
single version, nor was there a simple or single conclusion or lesson
that could be drawn from the stories. Rather, there was a vision, or
a range of visions.

   In *The View from the Cheap Seats*, Neil Gaiman comments that
"the forms of the tales that work survive, and the others die and are
forgotten."[8] But, as his observation implies, the tales take numerous
forms. If Gaiman calls his survival-of-the-fittest view "relentlessly
Darwinian," it is also the case that evolution throws up all kinds of
variegated life forms, even if most eventually go extinct.[9]

   Translating Euripides' poetry might be said to be another form
of un- and recrumpling; another way of changing the tale while also
keeping it the same; and another opportunity for engaging with a
powerful text. Many translations, some of them excellent, of these
durable plays exist already; I'm adding my own version to a rich
trove. What do I bring to this crowded table? In terms of my own
goals as a translator, I strove to maintain readability and colloquial
verve. However formal and stylized it is in the original, Greek tragedy needs to be dynamic and believable as speech. Euripides in par-
ticular is remote from the "suitably-attired-in-leather-boots/Head
of a traveler" mode of Housman's immortal parody;[10] he is urgent,

informal, clear. That said, in my rendering I tend not to sink below a certain level of diction. I tend, also, to avoid slang or profanity, not because I think slang or profanity is necessarily untrue to Euripides' debunking spirit but because I don't feel wholly comfortable writing in that register.

A second criterion I've kept in mind has been that the poetry of these plays (the dialogue portions as well as the choral odes and lyrics) should retain the intensity and pitch of—precisely—poetry. In this, I've been guided by my ear, as I am when I write my own poetry. Meter and rhyme help keep me on course and help maintain the pacing. My use of meter can be fluid, and I frequently use off-rhyme. But without some such formal constraints as rhyme and meter, I find that the language of the plays lacks the punch and condensation I always look for when I read poetry. It is a paradox of Euripides' style that the unbuttoned, often distinctly unheroic tenor of the personalities and action in his plays manages to coexist with language that is often chiseled, poised, and beautiful. I have tried to honor this paradox.

Finally, I hope that these two plays as I have rendered them are not only speakable but also actable. My 1995 translation of Euripides' *Helen*, as performed by the Verse Theater Company of Manhattan, was a lively Off-Broadway event; and my (still unpublished) rendering of Racine's *Iphigénie*, again produced by Verse Theater of Manhattan and performed in 2009 by Rutgers-Newark undergraduates as well as by professional actors, was also engaging.[11] The plots, or the one kaleidoscopic plot, of these plays are so durable that the words are a gift to the translator—or that has been my experience.

Notes

1. Lucretius, *De Rerum Natura, Book 1*, line 101.

2. James Merrill, "Unreal Citizen," in *Recitative: Prose by James Merrill*, ed. J. D. McClatchy (San Francisco: North Point Press, 1986), 99.

3. W. H. Auden, "In Memory of Sigmund Freud," in *W. H. Auden: Selected Poems*, ed. Edward Mendelson (New York: Vintage, 1992), 92.

4. Euripides, *Iphigenia in Tauris*, trans. Carolyn Kizer, in *Euripides, 4,* ed. David R. Slavitt and Palmer Bovie (Philadelphia: University of Pennsylvania Press, 1999).

5. Walt Whitman, "Song of the Exposition," in *Whitman: Poetry and Prose*, ed. Justin Kaplan (New York: Library of America, 1982), 342.

6. Tim Mayo, "Taxonomies," in *Thesaurus of Separation* (Montreal: Phoenicia Publishers, 2016).

7. Wallace Stevens, "Le Monocle de Mon Oncle," in *Harmonium* (London: Faber & Faber, 2001).

8. Neil Gaiman, *The View from the Cheap Seats: Selected Nonfiction* (New York: William Morrow, 2017), 59.

9. Gaiman, 42.

10. A. E. Housman, "Fragment of a Greek Tragedy," in *Unkind to Unicorns: Comic Verse of A. E. Housman*, ed. J. Roy Birch and Norman Page (Cambridge, England: Silent Books, 1995).

11. See Euripides, *Helen*, trans. Rachel Hadas, in *Euripides, 2*, ed. David R. Slavitt and Palmer Bovie (Philadelphia: University of Pennsylvania Press, 1998).

The Iphigenia Plays

Iphigenia in Aulis

CHARACTERS

AGAMEMNON, *king of Argos*

OLD MAN, *servant of Agamemnon*

CHORUS *of women from Euboea*

MENELAUS, *king of Sparta, brother of Agamemnon*

MESSENGER

CLYTEMNESTRA, *wife of Agamemnon*

IPHIGENIA, *daughter of Agamemnon and Clytemnestra*

ACHILLES, *leader of the Myrmidons*

SECOND MESSENGER

[*Scene: In front of* AGAMEMNON'*s tent in the Greek camp at Aulis, before dawn.*]

AGAMEMNON: Old man, come out here!

OLD MAN: Coming, coming! So
    what is it now, my king? Something new?

AGAMEMNON: Hurry. Now!

OLD MAN: Yes, yes, my king.
    I'm hurrying.
    I am too old to need
    sleep; but my eyes are still
    sharp. I come with speed.

AGAMEMNON: What dire star
    still high in the sky
    near the Pleiades
    is passing by?
    No sound of birdsong,
    no voice of the sea,
    no whisper of wind
    along the bay.

OLD MAN: Why did you dart out of your tent this way,
    Lord Agamemnon? It is not yet day.
    It's peaceful here in Aulis. All is still.
    The guards stand motionless—see?—on the wall.
    Let us go in.

AGAMEMNON: Old man, I envy you.
    I envy any human being who
    can get through their life in obscurity,
    unknown to fame.
    I do not envy people with a name,
    people in power.

OLD MAN: But fame and power are the best things in life.

AGAMEMNON: That best is too precarious. Such sweet
honors can cause suffering and regret.
Either we wish for what the gods deny,
or men's sharp tongues will have their painful say.

OLD MAN: Nobody in power should say such things.
Unmixed joy is not the fate of kings.
Agamemnon, you weren't born for bliss.
All mortals must both suffer and rejoice—
such is divine law, like it or not.

But now I see you write
a letter by lamplight.
You hold it in your hand
and then erase again
the words you have just written,
seal it and break the seal
and throw the pine frame down,
weeping. I see your tears.
I see you are distressed
almost to madness.
My king, what is your pain?
What terrible and new
matter troubles you?
Share your tale with me.
You know I'm a good man,
faithful and trustworthy—
Tyndareus' bridal gift
when you took Clytemnestra,
his daughter, as your wife.

AGAMEMNON: Thestius' daughter Leda gave birth to three
girls: Phoebe; Clytemnestra (my
wife) and Helen.

Around Helen swarmed the most
eligible young men of Greece—a host
of suitors. Threats and envy then ensued
for those who didn't win her when they wooed
beautiful Helen. What should Tyndareus do,
Helen's father? Should it be yes or no?
To bestow her hand in marriage, to deny
it—he would court disaster either way.
And then he had this thought: that all should swear,
with joined right hands and sacrifice and fire,
an oath to help each other, and to aid
whoever it should be that Helen married.
Should Helen be abducted from her home,
they swore to mount an expedition
to overthrow the city of that man,
be he Greek, be he barbarian.
Once they had sworn the oath (Tyndareus
guilefully encouraged them in this),
the father let his daughter have her choice.
Of suitors wafted toward Helen by Aphrodite's breeze,
Menelaus was the man she chose.
And this was a disastrous choice, I say.
For now from Troy
that judge of heavenly beauty,
or so tales say,
came to Sparta. He was himself a beauty,
shining with gold and barbarous luxury.
So these two fell in love, Helen and he.
And since Menelaus happened to be away,
Paris seized Helen, carried her to Troy
and to Mount Ida's pastures.
                           Mad with jealousy,
Menelaus called on all of Greece:
"Do not forget the oath you swore Tyndareus!"

Accordingly, Greek warriors armed themselves
and to the straits of Aulis rushed en masse,

with ships and shields, chariots and cavalry.
And for their general, who should they choose but me,
given that I am Menelaus' brother?
I wish to god they'd chosen any other
man but me. Here is why I say so:
we waited here for favoring winds to blow.
Till then we could not sail. So what to do?
Calchas the prophet, seeing our distress,
announced that we would have to sacrifice
Iphigenia, my daughter,
to Artemis, the goddess of this place;
that if we performed this sacrifice,
this slaughter,
we'd have the power to sail across the sea
and conquer Troy,
but if we should refuse,
then passage across the sea
and victory
would be denied to us.

When I heard this, I told Talthybius:
"Proclaim aloud my order to release
the army—let them all go home!" I could
not bear to slaughter my own flesh and blood.
But now Menelaus, cleverly
presenting many reasons, pressured me.
Here is what he persuaded me to do.
I wrote a letter, and I sent it, too,
telling my wife to send our daughter to
Aulis. Why? So she
could marry Achilles—what a lie!
I emphasized his high
position, stressed his nobility;
wrote that he'd never sail to Troy with us
unless he brought our daughter to his house
as his bride. This was the way that I
persuaded Clytemnestra—all a lie

about this marriage, for there will be none.
Calchas, Odysseus, and Menelaus alone
of all the Greeks are in this secret. But
I've reconsidered all the lies I wrote,
and in this second letter have revealed
(you saw me write, fold, seal it, and unfold)
to my wife how matters truly stand.
Now you must take this letter in your hand
and get yourself to Argos as quickly as you can.
All that I've written here I'll also say to you.
You are a faithful servant, that I know,
loyal to my wife and family too.

OLD MAN: Yes, please explain it all again to me
    so that what I say
    and this written letter will agree.

AGAMEMNON: "Daughter of Leda, I am sending you
    this second message: do
    not send our daughter here to Aulis' bay,
    safe from the waves, by the Euboean shore.
    We'll choose another season, time, and hour,
    altogether more
    auspicious, in which to solemnize
    our daughter's marriage vows."

OLD MAN: But won't Achilles, with an empty bed,
    roused to fury, turn on you instead,
    you and your wife? His anger
    is a dreadful danger.
    My lord, what do you say?

AGAMEMNON: I say Achilles' name alone is all we need.
    There is no wedding. This is word, not deed,
    and he knows nothing. I have never said
    that he could take my daughter to his bed
    as his bride, or that they could embrace.

OLD MAN: So then, my lord, you've dared a great disgrace,
    summoning your daughter here to wed
    the goddess's son, when all along instead
    you meant for her to die
    on the altar, a victim of the army!

AGAMEMNON: Oh god, my wits were wandering. I fell
    into a raging madness, dark as hell.
    Go, therefore, old man. Run!
    Go! Old age must not win.

OLD MAN: I go, I go, my king.

AGAMEMNON: No sitting in the shade to rest
    or halting by some spring.
    No napping.

OLD MAN: God forbid!

AGAMEMNON: Be vigilant! Especially
    where the road divides in two,
    no wagon rolling by
    must escape your eye—
    my daughter will be its passenger,
    coming toward the Greek ships, hurrying here.

OLD MAN: My lord, I understand. I shall obey.

AGAMEMNON: If you should meet
    her coming with her escorts, turn them back!
    Shake their reins and send them on their way
    home to the Cyclopean fortress of Mycenae.

OLD MAN: But if I do this, how can I appear
    trustworthy, faithful to your wife and daughter?

AGAMEMNON: Do not break the letter's seal. Now go.
    See—dawn's already glowing in the sky.
    The chariot of the sun is growing bright.
    Shoulder this burden. No man ever yet
    was always prosperous or fortunate.
    None of us is born
    to live free of pain.

[*Exit* OLD MAN. AGAMEMNON *goes back into his tent. The* CHORUS
*enters; separate choral members may be imagined as speaking singly in
the following passage.*]

CHORUS: Here we are
    on Aulis' shore,
    right across
    from the Euripus.
    We've left Calchis,
    our city, the nurse
    that feeds the spring of Arethousa—
    we've come to see
    the Greek army
    and all the ships.
    They are demigods, these Greeks!
    Blond Menelaus
    and noble Agamemnon,
    so our husbands tell us,
    are sending a fleet
    of a thousand ships
    to go after Helen.
    Paris the cowherd
    stole her from Sparta.
    She was Aphrodite's
    gift to Paris
    when the three goddesses,
    Hera, Athena, and Aphrodite,
    held their contest

by the bubbling spring:
who was the most beautiful?

I ran through the grove
of Artemis,
blushing with modesty,
red with excitement.
I wanted to see
the shields! the shelters!
I wanted to see
the Greeks in armor
and all the horses!
I saw both Ajaxes sitting there—
Ajax the son of Oileus,
and Ajax the son of Telamon,
who is the pride of Salamis.

I saw Protesilaus and Palamedes
(he is the grandson of Poseidon)
playing a board game in the sun,
playing with beautiful carved pieces.

I saw Diomedes throwing the discus
and standing next to him Meriones
(he is the son of the war god Ares).

I saw Laertes' son Odysseus,
the hero from that rocky island.

I saw Nireus, the handsomest
of all the Greeks.

The hero who can outrace the wind,
the runner Achilles, I saw him!
The goddess Thetis was his mother,
the centaur Chiron was his teacher.

I saw him running along the shore,
exercising in his armor,
racing a chariot with four horses,
darting ahead to victory.
Eumeles the charioteer,
grandson of Pheres, was shouting aloud
and whipping his beautiful gold-bridled horses.
The two in the middle had gray manes,
the outside pair had manes like fire
and dappled legs. The son of Peleus,
running his race, was keeping pace
with the wheels of the speeding chariot.

For the joy of feasting my greedy gaze,
I came to count the amazing ships.
On the right, the Myrmidons
from Phthia came in fifty ships,
Achilles' fleet—their figureheads
were gilded Nereids. Another fifty
ships from Argos were captained
by Euryalus and Sthenelos.

Commanded by the son of Theseus,
sixty ships had sailed from Athens;
their figurehead was the goddess Athena
on a chariot with winged horses,
high aloft above the sailors.

The Boeotians had fifty ships;
Cadmus, holding a golden serpent
high over the stern, was their figurehead.

Phocians, Locrians, so many others!

And from the stronghold of Mycenae,
built by Cyclopes, Agamemnon

son of Atreus had gathered warriors
enough to man a hundred ships
along with his brother Menelaus—
two kinsmen equal in command—
so Greece could punish the barbarians
who lured his wife out of her land.

Old warrior Nestor out of Pylos!

And the Aenians! And the Elians!
Captain Eurytus, Captain Meges.
Ajax of Salamis
with twelve ships
at the edge of the fleet—
I saw his crew.

Judging by what
I've heard and seen,
no barbarian
ships could conquer
our Greek fleet
and come safe home.

[*Enter* MENELAUS, *carrying the letter, pursued by the* OLD MAN.]

OLD MAN: Menelaus, how dare you do
    what you are doing?

MENELAUS: You're too loyal
    to your masters. Get away!

OLD MAN: Your blame for me is a source of pride.

MENELAUS: You will regret it if you do this deed!

OLD MAN: The letter I was carrying—you had the gall
    to snatch it!

MENELAUS: You've made trouble for us all.

OLD MAN: Tell that to others. Give it back to me!

[OLD MAN *tries to snatch the letter back from* MENELAUS.]

MENELAUS: I won't let go!

OLD MAN: Neither will I.

MENELAUS: I'll bash your head all bloody with my stick.

OLD MAN: Oh, what an honor, to die for my superiors!

MENELAUS: Quiet! Lackeys aren't supposed to give long speeches.

OLD MAN: Help, sir! He snatched your letter
        out of my hands by force, and he's threatening me.

[*Enter* AGAMEMNON.]

AGAMEMNON: Aha! What's going on out there?
        A brawl? Raised voices?

MENELAUS: I have more right to speak than he does.

AGAMEMNON: Menelaus, why are you threatening this old man?

MENELAUS: Here—look at this tablet first, then let me explain.

AGAMEMNON: Am I supposed to be afraid to see this?

MENELAUS: This tablet here? You know what it contains?
        You've read its shameful contents?

AGAMEMNON: I saw, I read. And the first thing for you
        is to let go of it. Give it to me.

MENELAUS: No! Not until every soldier in the army
　　understands every word this tablet says.

AGAMEMNON: So you've already read it. Have you learned
　　something you shouldn't know?

MENELAUS: Damn straight I've read it. Your classified information
　　has been exposed.

AGAMEMNON: Completely shameless. And when
　　did you happen to get your hands on it?

MENELAUS: While I was waiting for your daughter to arrive from
　　　Argos,
　　waiting to see if she would reach the army.

AGAMEMNON: What business is that of yours, you brazen bastard?

MENELAUS: I damn well felt like it.
　　And one more thing: remember I'm your equal.
　　I wasn't born a servant.

AGAMEMNON: Unbelievable. So I'm not allowed
　　to manage the affairs of my own household?

MENELAUS: No, you're not. And let me tell you why:
　　you are, you always were, and always will be
　　a devious weasel.

AGAMEMNON: 　　　　　Just who is devious? You have a talent
　　for prettifying what's abominable.

MENELAUS: And you have a talent for talking out of both sides of
　　　your mouth.
　　Your friends can never tell which side you're on.
　　But let me deconstruct the situation.
　　Stay here. Wait. Don't storm out.
　　I promise I'll be brief.

So. When
you were hot to lead the Greeks to Troy
(you didn't want to seem to be on fire
with ambition, but you know you were),
you were available to everyone—
hearty handshakes left and right,
office door never shut;
interviews granted whether people asked for them or not.
You were looking to be visible,
raise your profile, go up in every poll.

Then, when you took command—your heart's desire—
your friends found you less friendly than before.
You were no longer so accessible.
But when he's doing well,
exactly then a good man shouldn't change.
On the contrary,
he should help those who've shown him loyalty.
That's when you first disappointed me.

Then, when you got here,
commander of the whole fleet, you became
what? Nothing!
Fate dealt you a stunning blow
the day the gods blocked the favoring wind
needed to send the Greek fleet toward Troy.
So what to do?
The Greek army knew, or thought it knew:
abandon the expedition.
Forget the whole idea.
Don't waste one more day
waiting on the hopeless dream of Troy.

That spelled the end of your imaginings:
no more ships to command,
no soldiers swarming over Priam's land.
You turned (do you remember?) then to me:
"What should I do?

How do I escape this situation,
this hellish corner that I'm painted into?"
God forbid, you understand,
that you should lose your power and command,
honor, glory, fame, your burnished name.
Wait. I'm not done.
Then what?
Then, when
the prophet Calchas ordered you
to sacrifice your daughter
at Artemis' altar
so that the ships could sail across the water
to Troy, you were *relieved*
(don't say you were not—
finally a way out!)
and promised happily to do just that.
Of your own free will
you sent for the girl.
No one forced you to;
it was only you.
A marriage to Achilles was the lure
you used to bring her here,
to cover up the true
purpose of the altar
where she would meet no bridegroom except slaughter.

And now you've changed your mind a second time.
You wrote a letter
to countermand the order
for Iphigenia to come
to Aulis to her doom.
What could cause such a change?
How strange—
you do not wish to be
your daughter's murderer.
But, Agamemnon, this is how things are!
The sky, the sun, the air—

all have heard your word,
your solemn promise to sacrifice her.
You're caught.
There's no way out.
No, wait. Listen.
You're not the only one to fall a victim.
This happens to people all the time.
They bump up against obstacles, back down,
fail. Someone has made a bad decision.
There's some local revolution,
order gives way to dissolution.

As for me,
my heart bleeds, not for you, not for our family,
but for our country. Greece! Poor Greece!
We wanted to accomplish something glorious,
but the barbarians now will laugh at us,
all because of this business with your child.

Whether to sack a city or to lead
an army, it's not courage that you need,
but strategy: wit, brains.
Without intelligence, nothing remains.
For a man bereft
of ingenuity, there's nothing left.

CHORUS: It's a terrible thing when one
    brother blames the other.

AGAMEMNON: Now it is my turn to say a few
    hard truths to you—
    not arrogantly, but with sense and tact,
    as one brother to another.
    A decent man
    wants to proceed with caution
    and knows how to hold back.

So tell me: why are you on the attack,
huffing and puffing, purple in the face?
What is your problem? Who is hurting you?
You want a good wife, is that not true?
I can't help you there. The one you had—
let's say she didn't work out very well.
How is that my fault? What did I do wrong?

Nor is it my ambition that you hate.
No, nothing in my life
galls you. But you want a pretty wife
back in your arms, your bed—and so the hell
with moral standards. When a man turns vile,
even his pleasures are corrupt and foul.

I made a bad decision, I admit.
And now I've changed my mind. Does that
mean that I am crazy? No, it's you
who are raving, Menelaus—you who lost
a bad wife want her back at any cost.
The gods did you a favor when she went!
You know as well as I do, all the men
who hoped to marry Helen swore an oath
to Tyndareus. Come to think of it,
that hope precisely is the force at work here—
tougher by far than you,
stronger than any force you lead. So go—
march all those allied hopefuls into war.
Do you imagine such men's thoughts are clear?
The gods have sense and conscience. They see
when men who've sworn an oath
have done so wrongfully,
under compulsion, and when they have not.

I will not murder my own flesh and blood!
Why should you be happy in your life

once you have dealt out justice to your wife,
while I am worn away
with anguish and lie weeping night and day
because my children, innocent and good,
against all laws, sense, justice, piety,
are condemned to suffer? And why?
That's what I had to tell you, short and clear.
Do what you want to do. I no longer care.
Leave me to manage my own affairs.

CHORUS: His words this time strike quite a different note.
Not to kill one's own children—
it's hard for us to disagree with that.

MENELAUS: Where are all my friends?
No one is on my side.
No one seems to sympathize with me.

AGAMEMNON: You'll find friends when you act with decency.

MENELAUS: Since you act this way,
how can I know we're brothers, you and I?

AGAMEMNON: It's clear to me
we're brothers if you act with sanity.
Let's not show kinship with shared inhumanity.

MENELAUS: True kinship ought to mean we share the weight,
the burdens—

AGAMEMNON: Ask for something noble's sake.
I'll gladly help you with some worthy cause.
But don't ask me to help you break heaven's laws.

MENELAUS: So you've decided not to undergo
this agony for Greece's sake—

AGAMEMNON: No! You
     and Greece are suffering from one and the same
     heaven-sent misfortune.

MENELAUS: Brandish your scepter, then,
     flourish your kingship and betray your brother.
     I'll find some other way, I'll turn to other
     friends for help—

[*Enter* MESSENGER.]

MESSENGER: Ahem! Lord Agamemnon,
     commander in chief of all the Greeks, all hail! Here I am,
     having escorted your daughter and your wife from home,
     Iphigenia and Clytemnestra too,
     and—so that your cup can overflow
     with a father's joy—
     Orestes. You will see your little boy,
     you who've been absent for so long a time.

     Footsore and weary, they are resting now—
     I mean the ladies and the horses too.
     The mares are browsing in a field of green.
     I've come ahead, my lord, to make this known
     to you: rumor flies swiftly, and it's clear
     the army is aware your daughter's here.
     From every side the soldiers push and press,
     all for one glimpse of your daughter's face.
     Those whom fame and fortune have raised high
     are feasted on by every hungry eye.
     And that's not all. The army wants to know:
     Is Iphigenia to be married now?   .
     Is a wedding what this is about?
     Or could the loving king not do without
     his daughter, so he sent for her? Some say
     they'll dedicate the maiden
     to Artemis today.

Who will be her bridegroom?
All this is going on now. If you ask me,
ready the ritual immediately.
Strike up Hymen's hymn. Let dancing feet
and joyful voices be the sounds that greet
Iphigenia, and god bless the maid!

AGAMEMNON: Thank you for all this. Now step inside.
What will come next we'll let the Fates provide.

[*Exit* MESSENGER.]

Oh god, what to say and how to say it?
I can say
I'm cornered, trapped, yoked,
a crafty demon's prey.
Some dire divinity
has outwitted me.

Simple people are allowed to weep.
I envy them. They can say what they like,
no one cares. But we, the one percent,
we in high places have to keep
an eye on reputation.
We're slaves to how we seem.
So at a time like this—
what am I saying? I have never known
a time like this, this hideous nightmare time,
this awful dream of doom.

And now my wife has come.
How can I look at her?
What should I say?
What part am I supposed to play?
Her coming uninvited caps this catastrophe—
in the midst of dire emergency,
one more burden for me.

And yet of course a mother
wants to be near her daughter,
wants to attend the future bride.
What will Clytemnestra think of me,
playing the treacherous part I'll have to play?

And my poor child, poor girl, poor virgin—why
do I say "virgin"? Soon she'll marry death.
My heart bleeds for her. I
can hear the words she'll say:
"Father, you're going to kill me? Oh, may you
also marry death, destruction, doom—
you and anyone who's dear to you."
And I can hear Orestes crying too—
he's still a baby, but an infant's shrieks
can be more eloquent than adult speech.

Oh god, oh Helen's marriage,
oh Paris, Priam's son—
this is where your actions have led.
This is what you've done.
To this place you have brought us,
to this we've come.

CHORUS: I come from far away.
I am a stranger here.
No matter. It is clear
to me how much you have to bear,
what horrors you, a king, will now endure.

MENELAUS: Brother, give me your hand.

AGAMEMNON: Take it. You're strong; I'm miserable and weak.

[MENELAUS *and* AGAMEMNON *clasp hands.*]

MENELAUS: By our grandfather Pelops let me swear
and by our father Atreus—I will speak
from the heart, I'll say it loud and clear,
no sidewinding, nothing but what I think.
When I saw you weep, I felt for you
and I wept too.
So, brother, now I'm stepping back
from what I said before.
Trust me: I will threaten you no more.
Why should I want to add to what you fear?
Now I am where you are.
And now I say to you: do not
kill your child. Do not
in her place take my child's life instead.
Why should you spend your life in agony
while I live mine in joy?
It's cruel, it's unjust, it isn't right—
your child to die while mine still sees the light?

And after all, I ask myself, what is it that I want?
Say marriage, a good marriage, is my goal—
well, that's attainable,
that's an ambition that I can fulfill.
But to destroy
my brother, who should be
most near and dear to me—
to prefer Helen, choose her over you?
I was young and thoughtless then, I know.
I never thought it through,
never imagined how it might feel
to do this thing, to kill
one's own child.
And then—
then pity woke in me
for the poor girl (who's after all my niece)
whose destiny is: be a sacrifice—

and to my marriage? She will die for that?
That makes no sense!
What does your daughter have to do with Helen?
Cancel the expedition!
Scrub the invasion! Let the army go
home! Stop weeping, brother,
and please stop asking me to weep for you.
And one more thing—if you have any share
in these oracles, these murky bulletins
about your daughter, count me out.
You are welcome to them. Take mine too.
I want nothing more to do
with any of that.

So have I changed my tune,
stepped back from the brink of dreadful speech?
In loving you, my brother,
born of the same father
as I, and the same mother,
I've finally understood
how decent men act. I've embraced the good.

CHORUS: You've spoken nobly, so as not to shame
   your noble forebears. You deserve no blame.

AGAMEMNON: I praise you, Menelaus. Past my hope
   you chose the right words just now when you spoke.
   Turmoil between brothers comes from lust—
   for a woman, for an inheritance.
   I reject all such bitterness. I spew
   it out of my mouth—and so, I see, do you.
   But we've arrived at fate's sheer edge now, brother,
   hideous and merciless—to slaughter
   my own daughter.

MENELAUS: But how? What man could ever force you to?

AGAMEMNON: Massed manpower, the Greek army—that's who.

MENELAUS: No,
     not if you send your daughter home again.

AGAMEMNON: That part I might conceal; the other, not.

MENELAUS: Not what?
     You shouldn't be too fearful of the crowd.

AGAMEMNON: Calchas will shout his oracles aloud
     to the whole army.

MENELAUS: Not if he is dead,
     he won't. He can't.

AGAMEMNON: Curse the whole teeming breed
     of prophets, all corrupted by their greed.

MENELAUS: Useless when they're most needed; and whenever
     they are of any use, the outcome's bitter.

AGAMEMNON: Aren't you afraid of what it is I've planned?

MENELAUS: You've told me nothing. I can't read your mind.

AGAMEMNON: But Sisyphus' descendant knows of this.
     He understands it all.

MENELAUS: Odysseus?
     Surely he presents no threat to us.

AGAMEMNON: No threat? The man is a chameleon.
     Impossible to gauge which side he's on,
     except he leans toward the majority.

MENELAUS: And his ambition threatens us—I see.

AGAMEMNON: How can you not imagine he will stand
    and shout to all the soldiers on the ground,
    spilling out Calchas' secret words to them—
    the sacrifice I swore I'd make, and then
    I ate my words, took back my oath again?
    How can you not see that Odysseus
    will seize control and murder both of us,
    then finally, as commander, give the order
    to sacrifice my daughter? Say I flee
    to Argos—then the army follows me
    to the ramparts, the ancient citadel,
    the Cyclopean stones that crown the hill.
    They'll break in, plunder and destroy the place.
    Gods, I foresee destruction and disgrace.
    You have taken all my power away.

    There's one thing, brother, that you still have power
    to do: canvass the army and make sure
    that my wife Clytemnestra doesn't know
    any of this. Alone I must bestow
    my daughter on her pale groom down below.
    At least I will shed fewer tears that way.
    You foreign women too I swear to secrecy.

[*Exit* MENELAUS, AGAMEMNON, *and* OLD MAN.]

CHORUS: Blessed are the cautious! Know
    Eros has twin arrows for his bow.
    One shoots delight with moderation,
    the other passion's hot frustration.
    O lovely Cyprian goddess, keep
    blond Eros far from where I sleep.
    May my joys all be restrained,
    may all my pleasures be contained.
    Let me sip love's cup carefully
    and never drain it greedily.

People differ naturally,
but what is noble is clear to see.
If they are taught
to do what's right,
to a shrewd feel for what to do
they add a sense of modesty.
What other people think of you
brings a good name and lasting fame.
Order and virtue benefit
city and citizens and state.
As a cowherd you were raised,
Paris, on Mount Ida's slopes,
playing Asian tunes on your pipes
while peacefully the cattle grazed.
The competition there took place
that would send you off to Greece,
the beauty contest known to all—
no need to tell it or retell.
Enough to say that's how you came
to stand before the ivory throne
of Helen. As you gazed into
each other's eyes, love conquered you
and equally love conquered her.

So, Paris, you have brought us here.
Greece gathered ships and gathered men
massed to sail across to Troy
and destroy her citadel
and bring Helen home again.

[*Enter* CLYTEMNESTRA *and* IPHIGENIA.]

All hail to the fortunate,
the queenly, and the truly great:
Iphigenia and her mother,
Tyndareus' noble daughter
Clytemnestra—a royal race

whose destiny holds a lofty place.
They must be gods, they seem so great
to us who are less fortunate.

People of Chalcis, here we stand.
Receive our queen with gentle hand
as you guide her down from her chariot
and she touches our soil with regal feet.
Take extra care
of the princess there—
Iphigenia, a stranger here,
newly arrived and far from home.
Strangers ourselves, we're greeting strangers.
May you be welcome and free from danger.

CLYTEMNESTRA: Your gracious welcome strikes the proper note.
A noble marriage brings me here, I hope,
in my role as escort to the bride.
This dowry I have brought—take it inside,
carry these gifts into the tent with care.
And you, my daughter, leave the chariot. There,
set your foot down gently on the ground.
Young women, catch her, please, as she steps down.
I too need support as I descend—
will some one of you kindly lend a hand?
You others, stand before the horses. They
must be soothed, or they might bolt and shy.

This little boy here, Agamemnon's son,
take him in your arms and lift him down.
The chariot was your cradle, love; you're sleeping
still, but you'll wake to see your sister's wedding.
Noble yourself, you'll gain a lordly brother,
godlike Achilles. Thetis was his mother.
Iphigenia, come stand here next to me
so we may greet these women whom you see.
And you must speak to your dear father too.

Ladies, can you tell me whether my
husband Lord Agamemnon is nearby?

CHORUS: Here he is. You see he's coming toward us.

[*Enter* AGAMEMNON.]

IPHIGENIA: Mother, please let me run ahead of you
and hug Daddy and let him hug me.

CLYTEMNESTRA: My master Agamemnon and my lord,
you see we've come, obedient to your word.

IPHIGENIA: Let me throw my arms around you now,
Daddy! How long it's been. I love you so.
Do not be angry.

CLYTEMNESTRA: Yes, my daughter, that is how it must
be. You always loved your father most
of all our children.

IPHIGENIA: It has been so long!
Oh, I'm so glad to see you!

AGAMEMNON: And I you,
my child. This joy of yours—I feel it too.

IPHIGENIA: How right you were to bring me here!

AGAMEMNON: Right or wrong, it isn't all that clear.

IPHIGENIA: Why? Oh Father, now you look so sad.

AGAMEMNON: Kings and generals are preoccupied.

IPHIGENIA: Here now with me, forget your worries, do.

AGAMEMNON: See? I am nowhere else. I'm all with you.

IPHIGENIA: Then smooth your face and wipe that frown away.

AGAMEMNON: I'm happy that you're here. I'm smiling. See?

IPHIGENIA: Why are your eyes wet, then?

AGAMEMNON: Because so
long it will be—my time apart from you.

IPHIGENIA: Father dear, please help me understand.
The Phrygians—where is their native land?

AGAMEMNON: Where I wish Paris never had been born.

IPHIGENIA: You're traveling far and leaving me alone.

AGAMEMNON: You grasp the situation. Since you do,
I feel all the more pity for us two.

IPHIGENIA: Maybe I should talk nonsense—would that cheer
you up? Oh Daddy—

AGAMEMNON: Oh, the pain! My dear—
[*Aside*] Not to be able to tell her—

IPHIGENIA: Father, stay
with your children. Don't go far away.

AGAMEMNON: I want to stay. I can't. That tortures me.

IPHIGENIA: Spears, weapons—why can't they just go away?
And Menelaus' anger—

AGAMEMNON: —which will destroy
others after it has ruined me.

IPHIGENIA: You've lingered here in Aulis now for so
    long—

AGAMEMNON: Yes, and even now we cannot go.

IPHIGENIA: If only I could sail away with you!

AGAMEMNON: You will be voyaging too, and to a place
    where you will forget your father's face.

IPHIGENIA: Will Mother come, or will I sail alone?

AGAMEMNON: No father and no mother. On your own.

IPHIGENIA: Will you be settling me in a new home?

AGAMEMNON: Young girls shouldn't know these things. No more!

IPHIGENIA: Please hurry home from Troy when you're done there.

AGAMEMNON: I must perform a sacrifice first here.

IPHIGENIA: What rites, what rituals will you obey?

AGAMEMNON: You will be standing by, so you will see.

IPHIGENIA: And will we girls be standing round the altar?

AGAMEMNON: If only I knew none of this, my daughter!
    But young girls should be modest. Go on in.
    Give me a kiss first, let me squeeze your hand—
    you will be far from me a long, long time.
    Oh youthful face and body, golden hair,
    Troy and Helen cause us such despair!
    Go in now quickly. I can say no more.
    I'm weeping as I hug you.

[*Exit* IPHIGENIA.]

                              Pardon me,
daughter of Leda, if excessively
I may have mourned at giving her away,
our daughter, to Achilles. Yes, I know
parents are blessed when they can bestow
a child so well. Yet it is painful too
to raise a child, then send her far away.

CLYTEMNESTRA: I understand your feelings. And I too,
when the moment comes, will feel like you,
leading our daughter with the wedding hymn.
The man who'll be our son-in-law—his name
I know, but not his family or home.

AGAMEMNON: The river god Asopus sired a daughter,
Aigina.

CLYTEMNESTRA: And what god or man then sought her
hand in marriage?

AGAMEMNON: A god. lt was Zeus
who married her and fathered Aeacus,
Oenone's husband.

CLYTEMNESTRA: And which son of his
was heir to his estates?

AGAMEMNON: Lord Peleus.
And Peleus married Nereus' daughter.

CLYTEMNESTRA: With a god's blessing? Or perhaps he took her
by force?

AGAMEMNON: Not by force. Zeus, her lord, bestowed her hand.

CLYTEMNESTRA: And was the ceremony on dry land
  or underwater?

AGAMEMNON: Deep in the sacred glen
  of Pelion. Chiron lives there.

CLYTEMNESTRA: There where men
  say the race of centaurs have their halls?

AGAMEMNON: The gods chose there for Peleus' nuptials.

CLYTEMNESTRA: Did Thetis raise Achilles, her son,
  or did his father Peleus?

AGAMEMNON: Neither one.
  Chiron the centaur shielded him from men
  and mortal mischief.

CLYTEMNESTRA: That was wisely done
  by the parents and the teacher too.

AGAMEMNON: Such is the man our child is given to.

CLYTEMNESTRA: I find no fault. What place does he call home?

AGAMEMNON: In Phthia, near the Apidanus stream.

CLYTEMNESTRA: He'll bring her there, this virgin girl of ours?

AGAMEMNON: Leave that to him who'll take her to his house.

CLYTEMNESTRA: May all go well for them! The wedding's when?

AGAMEMNON: With the completed cycle of the moon.

CLYTEMNESTRA: The ritual offerings—have these been seen to?

AGAMEMNON: I am precisely on that business now.

CLYTEMNESTRA: You'll put the wedding feast off for a time?

AGAMEMNON: Yes; this sacrifice has a prior claim.

CLYTEMNESTRA: Where shall we hold the women's ritual feast?

AGAMEMNON: Near where the ships are, right here on the beach.

CLYTEMNESTRA: A bad choice, and unworthy. Still, I pray
all will be well.

AGAMEMNON: What you must do: obey.
My will is law, and everything I say.

CLYTEMNESTRA: I've learned to be obedient, my dear.

AGAMEMNON: And as for us, when once the bridegroom's here—

CLYTEMNESTRA: What will you do that a mother should have done?

AGAMEMNON: —among the soldiers we will marry her.

CLYTEMNESTRA: Where will I be while this is taking place?

AGAMEMNON: At home in Argos, managing our house
and family.

CLYTEMNESTRA: Leave my child? But who will light
the bridal torch?

AGAMEMNON: I will do what is right.
Whatever the groom needs, I'll see to it.

CLYTEMNESTRA: Against all custom? All of this seems wrong.

AGAMEMNON: Nor is it right for you to linger long
    here amidst the army.

CLYTEMNESTRA: But I say
    it is my right to give my child away,
    the daughter I gave birth to.

AGAMEMNON: But your other
    children you leave at home? You're not the mother
    of just one daughter.

CLYTEMNESTRA: They are safe at home!

AGAMEMNON: Listen to me!

CLYTEMNESTRA: I swear by Hera, queen
    of Argos, I will run affairs within
    the house. You rule the world, but leave to me
    management inside our family.
    I know what I must do and what brides need.

[*Exit* CLYTEMNESTRA.]

AGAMEMNON: Gods, what a failure! Everything I've tried—
    to get my wife away from here; to trick
    my loved ones—nothing works, nothing will stick.
    I've nowhere left to turn in my defeat
    except to the priest Calchas—he and I
    cooperate in brewing misery
    for all of Greece; for me, catastrophe.
    Marry a good wife or else live alone.
    Better by far than a bad wife is none.

[*Exit* AGAMEMNON.]

CHORUS: The whole Greek army will come,
    come with ships and weapons,

come to the silvery river,
to rocky Troy, the city Apollo built.

Cassandra crowned with myrtle
tosses her golden hair
whenever from the gods
the power of prophecy
blows into her, gusts through her.

With his bronze shield the war god
will stride across the sea,
trying to bring back Helen,
Castor and Pollux's sister,
back with the army's help,
back to her country, Greece.
Ranged along the walls
and on their city's towers,
the Trojans will stand and stare.

The war god will surround
Troy with its towers of stone—
throats cut, heads chopped off,
the city sacked and wrecked,
destroyed from top to bottom.
The virgin girls will scream
and Priam's wife will weep.

The cause of all this wailing,
Helen, Zeus's daughter,
will come to learn the cost
of having left her husband.
Oh may no breath, no rumor,
no slightest tremor ever
reach me or touch my children,
such as the wealthy men of Troy
felt, and the Trojan women,

sitting at their looms,
murmuring to each other:
"What man will pull me screaming,
will drag me by the hair,
tear me from my city,
uproot me from my country?
And all because of you,
daughter of the swan,
if what they say is true
and Leda gave birth to you,
having lain with Zeus
when he took another form—
unless the Muses tell
mortals a fairy tale."

[*Enter* ACHILLES.]

ACHILLES: Where's the Greek high commander? And will one
　　of his aides inform him Peleus' son
　　Achilles now awaits
　　him right here at the gates?

　　What are we doing here but marking time?
　　Unmarried men have left their homes alone,
　　deserted, and sit waiting by the sea;
　　others have left a wife and family.
　　So powerful and fearful is the lust
　　the gods have planted in each Hellene's breast,
　　so dreadful the desire
　　for this war.

　　Others can tell you how it seems to them.
　　Here is how I see my situation:
　　I left my native land of Thessaly,
　　I left my father Peleus far away.
　　Now I sit idle as my Myrmidons

press me: "Achilles, what are we waiting for?
How long will we be stalled here on the shore?
How lengthy will this expedition be,
this strange war against Troy?
If there is any deed for you to do,
do it—or take the army home with you.
But no more waiting here for Atreus' sons
to stir their timid bones."

[*Enter* CLYTEMNESTRA.]

CLYTEMNESTRA: Son of the water nymph, I heard your voice,
    so I have ventured out here from the house.

ACHILLES: I don't think we're acquainted. Who are you?
    I see you're beautiful and modest too.

CLYTEMNESTRA: No wonder, never having seen me, you
    don't recognize me. But my modesty
    you praise; for that I praise you.

ACHILLES: But who are you? What are you doing here? Why
    a woman in the middle of the army?

CLYTEMNESTRA: I'm Clytemnestra, Leda's daughter, wife
    of Agamemnon.

ACHILLES: Well put—clear and brief.
    But I can't stay
    here gossiping this way
    with a woman. You must understand
    to do this is disgraceful—

CLYTEMNESTRA: Take my hand!
    Don't run away. Come back! We'll inaugurate
    the blessings of the blissful married state.

ACHILLES: What are you saying? Take your right hand? Me?
    And then look Agamemnon in the eye,
    having done what I had no right to do?

CLYTEMNESTRA: No right? But every right belongs to you,
    son of the goddess who lives underwater.
    Achilles, you are marrying my daughter!

ACHILLES: Marrying? What the—woman, I'm struck dumb.
    No, you must be insane. These ravings come
    from madness—

CLYTEMNESTRA: Oh, I understand. You're shy.
    It's natural. Anyone would feel this way—
    new faces, in-laws, whole new family.

ACHILLES: Marrying your daughter never crossed my mind,
    woman. I never tried to win her hand.
    Her father and uncle never said a word.

CLYTEMNESTRA: Let's try to understand what we've just heard.
    You and I are at a total loss.

ACHILLES: The same bewilderment stuns both of us,
    both of us equally confused by lies.

CLYTEMNESTRA: What's happening? It seems I came to chase
    a phantom marriage. Gods, what a disgrace.

ACHILLES: Someone seems to have made fools of us two.
    Let's simply disregard it, I and you.

CLYTEMNESTRA: I can't stay here. Good-bye! I lied to you
    unwittingly, since they lied to me too.

ACHILLES: My sentiments exactly. Let me go
    inside to see your husband.

[*Enter* OLD MAN.]

OLD MAN: Wait! Yoo-hoo,
    son of the goddess! And you, Leda's child!

ACHILLES: Who's calling from the doorway? He seems wild
    with terror.

OLD MAN: I'm a slave. That is the long
    and short of it.

ACHILLES: To whom do you belong?
    Not to me. What's Agamemnon's is
    Agamemnon's; what is mine's not his.

OLD MAN: This lady by the gate—you see her here—
    I was a gift from her father to her.

ACHILLES: What do you want? You're standing in my way.

OLD MAN: Is there nobody here besides you two?

ACHILLES: No one but us, so come on out of there.

OLD MAN: May luck and wit save those I care for!

ACHILLES: Yes,
    I'll second that, old man. Nevertheless,
    you're slow to tell your story.

OLD MAN: Lady, give
    me your right hand. I count on you to save
    me from destruction.

CLYTEMNESTRA: My right hand is here.
    What do you have to tell me? Do not fear.

OLD MAN: First, do you understand my loyalty
    for years past to you and your family?

CLYTEMNESTRA: You are an old retainer, that I know.

OLD MAN: When Lord Agamemnon married you,
    I was a wedding gift.

CLYTEMNESTRA: You came with me
    to Argos, stayed, and served the family.

OLD MAN: Exactly; and I'm loyal to you still,
    your husband not so much.

CLYTEMNESTRA: Tell me! Reveal
    what has been hidden.

OLD MAN: It's this: your husband plans
    to kill your child and his with his own hands—

CLYTEMNESTRA: What? You are raving. I spit out your words.

OLD MAN: —slitting her white throat with a bloody sword.

CLYTEMNESTRA: Has he lost his mind? What shall I do?

OLD MAN: He's sane, my lady,
    except when it comes to you and to your daughter.

CLYTEMNESTRA: But why? What crazy vengeance is this?

OLD MAN: It is what the priest Calchas prophesies,
    so that the army can go—

CLYTEMNESTRA: —can go where?
    Poor child, your father is a murderer!

OLD MAN: —can go to Troy, so Menelaus can
     bring Helen home.

CLYTEMNESTRA: So Helen's return spells my daughter's doom?

OLD MAN: That's it exactly. And your husband is
     preparing as we speak to sacrifice
     the girl to Artemis.

CLYTEMNESTRA: But the marriage, then?
     The wedding plans that brought me here from home?

OLD MAN: A ruse—so that you'd willingly
     bring her to be
     Achilles' bride.

CLYTEMNESTRA: My daughter—now I see
     destruction here awaits both you and me.

OLD MAN: I sense what you're both suffering, she and you.
     A dreadful deed Agamemnon has dared to do.

CLYTEMNESTRA: Oh, let me weep! Oh god, my misery!

OLD MAN: To lose one's child—that is the greatest grief.
     Weep, my lady. May tears bring relief.

CLYTEMNESTRA: How did you learn of this? I need to know.

OLD MAN: A letter I was to deliver to you
     earlier—

CLYTEMNESTRA: You mean a letter urging me to bring
     my daughter here, or halting everything?

OLD MAN: Do *not* bring her was what the letter said.
     Agamemnon then had not yet lost his head.

CLYTEMNESTRA: You never gave this letter to me. Why?

OLD MAN: Because Menelaus snatched it away from me.
	He is responsible for this disaster.

CLYTEMNESTRA: Son of the nymph and Peleus, do you hear?

ACHILLES: I hear that you are wretched. And I too
	am an offended party here.

CLYTEMNESTRA: Her marriage to you
	was nothing but a trick! They will slaughter
	my daughter!

ACHILLES: Your husband Agamemnon is to blame.
	I will not take this insult lying down.

[CLYTEMNESTRA *kneels.*]

CLYTEMNESTRA: A mortal to a goddess's son—you see,
	Achilles, how I bend my knee to you?
	My daughter is all I care about, so you,
	goddess-born, I beg you: help me now.
	Even if she was said to be your bride
	by heartless men who lied
	knowingly, it was for you I brought her,
	wreathed and veiled, here—to what kind of altar?
	For you it would be everlasting shame,
	a blot upon the brilliance of your name,
	to fail to help me now. You never wed,
	but you were called her husband—so they said.
	So I implore you, by your chin, your hand,
	your mother! I've no help, no place to stand.
	There is no altar to which I can flee.
	All I can do is kneel and touch your knee.
	I have no friends here. Agamemnon—you
	see how he is, wild, cruel, and impious too.

I've ventured here, a woman, I alone,
to face a lawless navy on my own.
They're bold, but bold for evil. Dare extend
your hand on my behalf, my only friend.
Otherwise I am lost.

CHORUS: To be a mother is strong medicine—
loving, more than loving, living for
your children—shared by everyone
who's given birth.

ACHILLES: I'm touched. But the right way
to share both griefs and joys is moderately.
Only people who employ their sense
can live their lives out with intelligence.
Not overthinking offers us some pleasure,
but cleverness is good in equal measure.
Raised in holy Chiron's household, I
have studied virtue and simplicity.
So if the sons of Atreus lead the way
to virtuous action, then I shall obey;
if not, then not. In Aulis and in Troy,
my spirit must be unrestrained and free
so that my spear can honor the god of war.

But you, maltreated by those near and dear
to you, I pity you. And I promise this:
your daughter never will be sacrificed
by her father. She's been called my bride.
I won't allow myself to be ensnared
in the net your husband has prepared.
My name is not a weapon; yet my name
will be your daughter's killer all the same,
through Agamemnon's plot. And I would lose
my purity and virtue if through this
marriage Iphigenia were to die,
having already suffered terribly,

victim of an abominable trick.
What would that make me? Merely one more Greek,
a Menelaus, a mediocrity,
amounting to just this: a nobody,
no son of Peleus but murder's son,
since in my name the murder will be done.
No! By my grandfather Nereus I swear
(he sired my mother Thetis and raised her
under the sea), your lord won't touch a hair
of Iphigenia's head. I will not let
him graze her robe's hem with his fingertip
If I am wrong, the Atreidae will preen
their lineage from Sipylos, their fame,
while Phthia will be a forgotten name,
my native land! And Calchas should take care
with those libations of his. Let him beware,
this prophet! What is a prophet, anyway?
Someone who speaks the truth occasionally
but much more often lies, and when it's clear
that he's been lying, he will disappear.
I don't say this from any wish to be
a bridegroom—countless girls would marry me!
But Agamemnon's insult has brought shame
on what he never asked me for: my name.
To trap his child, he used my name as bait,
and also drew his wife into the net.
If the Greek host had had a real need
of me to help them sail, I'd have agreed
to help the cause, to serve the common weal.
But now I'm nothing. Badly treated, well
treated—no, the generals do not care.
So by my sword I swear:
it will drip blood before I get to Troy
if someone tries to take my bride away.
Calm your fears, my lady; trust in me,
in my divine blood, in epiphany.

CHORUS: Noble words, son of Peleus, you have said,
  and worthy of your mother's godly blood.

CLYTEMNESTRA: Oh god,
  I fear to speak too many or too few
  words of praise and gratitude to you.
  When virtuous men are praised beyond all measure,
  they come to hate the praise that should give pleasure.
  And telling my sad story, I feel shame.
  It's my misfortune; you are not to blame.
  Yet it is also true
  that a good man should be attentive to
  (even from a distance) other people's woe.
  We're miserable. Take pity on us, then!
  First I thought that you would be my son-
  in-law: an empty hope. And secondly
  my child's death would be a black blot on you
  and any future marriage you may make.
  This you must avoid, for both your sakes.
  I liked your speech's start, and its end too.
  Save my daughter's life! It's up to you.
  Do you desire her to embrace your knees?
  Although that is immodest, if you please
  she'll put aside all shame. But I prefer
  she stay inside, not in the open here.
  Better to maintain one's dignity
  and hope to be treated with courtesy.
  Still, self-respect can be a luxury.

ACHILLES: No, do not bring her out to see my face.
  Better not to expose her to disgrace.
  The gathered army, far from homes and wives,
  breeds vicious gossip about others' lives.
  Whether you entreat me or do not,
  my goal is saving you from this vile fate.
  You've heard me say this, and I do not lie.
  If I don't speak the truth now, may I die!

But may I not die; may I rather be
alive and well to save your daughter.

CLYTEMNESTRA: Oh,
may praise and blessings continually flow
on you who help the wretched!

ACHILLES: Lady, now,
so all may go well, listen carefully.

CLYTEMNESTRA: Whatever you command, I will obey.

ACHILLES: First of all, we must try again to bring
back to his senses this war-maddened king.

CLYTEMNESTRA: No; he's a coward and a weakling, who
fears the army.

ACHILLES: Yes; but reason too
has the power
to conquer fear.

CLYTEMNESTRA: A chilly hope. But I'll do what you say.

ACHILLES: Begin, then, by begging him not to slay
his child. If he refuses, turn to me.
If he agrees, persuasion wins the day
and saves her life; I prove a faithful friend;
the army will not fault me; words prevail
over violence. If this plan goes well,
your difficulties vanish without me—
a joy to you and to your family.

CLYTEMNESTRA: Wise words. I will obey.
I will do what you say.
But if this plan should fail, where will you be

for me to turn to in my misery,
to reach for your strong hand to rescue me?

ACHILLES: A guard is needed, and I will be he.
No one must see you rush hysterically
through the army. You must not bring shame
on the luster of Tyndareus' name.

CLYTEMNESTRA: So be it. Rule! Decide!
Be the leader; I will follow.
If the gods' claim to justice isn't hollow,
you will be victorious. Otherwise,
why should we struggle all our mortal days?

[*Exit* CLYTEMNESTRA *and* ACHILLES.]

CHORUS: Wedding music: Libyan flute,
cithara that loves the dance,
pan pipes, cries of "Ahhh!"
The Pierian Muses with beautiful hair,
stamping their gold-sandaled feet,
came to the slopes of Pelion,
Centaur Mountain, and sang the hymn
to celebrate the wedding feast
of Peleus and Thetis. And
the delight of Zeus's bed,
the young Trojan Ganymede
from the mixing bowl poured wine
into cups of shining gold.
On the brilliant white sand
Nereus' fifty daughters
twirled in circles round and round
to celebrate the wedding feast.

Crowned with green leaves and clutching pine boughs,
a troop of centaurs came clattering
up to the brimming vats of wine.

Aloud they shouted: "Daughter of Nereus,
Chiron our prophet, the centaur Chiron,
Chiron who knows Apollo's song,
proclaims that you will bear a son,
a great light to Thessaly.

And with his fighting Myrmidons
he will march on Priam's land,
invade the city, burn it down,
wearing the gift his mother gave him,
golden armor Hephaestus made."

The gods showered blessings on that union,
the marriage of Peleus
to the eldest Nereid.
But you, virgin girl—
as if you were a mountain doe,
as if you were a spotless heifer,
the Greeks will tie a garland on your head.
They'll slice your perfect throat
and blood will flow.
You weren't raised
to be a shepherdess,
your background music the crude
toot-tooting of a pipe.
No, your mother came escorting you
to your destiny: a princely marriage.

Gods! Any human sense of shame
or virtuous action is all gone.
Power flows to what's unholy,
and good behavior sadly trails
behind, neglected. Lawlessness
trumps all human decency.
No mortals even try
to avoid divine ill will,
to ward off the gods' envy.

[*Enter* CLYTEMNESTRA.]

CLYTEMNESTRA: My husband has been missing a long time.
    I've come out here
    to find him. And our daughter, now she knows
    what sort of doom her father has devised,
    fills the air
    with her despair
    and with appalling cries.
    Here comes my husband, whose unholy plot
    against his own child soon will be found out.

[*Enter* AGAMEMNON.]

AGAMEMNON: Daughter of Leda, I'm glad to find you here
    outside the house. Our child should not be near
    to overhear a message no young bride should hear.

CLYTEMNESTRA: What is your message? What's the urgent need?

AGAMEMNON: To bring the girl outside.
    The holy water's ready,
    the barley's ready too,
    to throw into the fire
    to be purified.
    The heifers are at hand
    that must be sacrificed
    before the wedding feast.
    Artemis is thirsty. She wants blood.

[*Enter* IPHIGENIA.]

CLYTEMNESTRA: The words you're speaking signal that all's well;
    the truth is that you're planning something vile.
    Come out, my child. You know
    what it is your father means to do.
    And bring your little brother out with you,

Orestes—that's it, yes,
enfold him in a corner of your dress.
Here she is, obedient and demure.
Henceforth I'll speak both for myself and her.

AGAMEMNON: My child, why weep?
Come look me in the face.
Why do you keep
your gaze fixed on the ground
or cover your eyes
with a fold of your dress?

CLYTEMNESTRA: Oh god, the horror—where should I begin?
The start, the end, the middle—all spell pain.

AGAMEMNON: What is it? On each face I see the same
look of panic and confusion.

CLYTEMNESTRA: I need to ask you something. Answer me,
I beg you, truthfully.

AGAMEMNON: Question me. I don't require commanding.

CLYTEMNESTRA: To kill our child—is that what you are planning?

AGAMEMNON: Dreadful. Unspeakable. Do not say such a thing.

CLYTEMNESTRA: Stay calm and answer me. I ask again.

AGAMEMNON: Ask reasonable questions; my reply
will also be reasonable.

CLYTEMNESTRA: Agreed: I
will ask you fairly. Fairly answer me.

AGAMEMNON: Oh fate and luck and my divinity—

CLYTEMNESTRA: Yours, mine, and hers. Three people; one ill fate.

AGAMEMNON: Who has wronged you?

CLYTEMNESTRA: How can you ask me that?
    You cannot sustain even your own plot.
    Your cleverness is feeble. It has failed.

AGAMEMNON: I've been betrayed. My secret is revealed.

CLYTEMNESTRA: Yes, I have learned what you intend to do.
    Your sighs, your silence—both confess to me.
    No lengthy answers, please. Don't even try.

AGAMEMNON: See? I am silent. If I tell a lie,
    shamelessness adds to this catastrophe.

CLYTEMNESTRA: Listen to me, then, and you will hear
    language like prose—
    that simple and that clear,
    no riddles or distortions to disguise
    the truth. No lies.
    First in my catalogue of blame is this:
    you took me and you married me by force,
    murdering my first husband, Tantalus,
    and ripping my young infant from my breast.
    Castor and Pollux, sons of Zeus, my two
    brothers, galloped in to rescue me;
    Tyndareus, my old father, heard your plea
    and took your side, and so you married me.
    And so we lived. Of our domestic life,
    you must admit I was a perfect wife,
    moderate in passion, one who always cared
    to sustain the household that we shared
    so you could enjoy your privacy
    and in the wider world prosperity.

A wife like me is very hard to find;
there is no shortage of the other kind.
I gave birth to three girls, and to this boy.
And one of my children you dare take from me?
If someone should ever ask you why,
what—I ask you—would your answer be?
Shall I speak for you? "So Menelaus may
win Helen back." Too high a price to pay,
your own offspring to suffer such a fate,
to barter what you love for what you hate!

You go to war and leave me here alone.
For all the dragging time that you'll be gone,
can you imagine how I'll feel? Despair
each time I see my daughter's empty chair,
her empty room. Try to imagine me
weeping for her loss incessantly.
What shall I say?
"Daughter, the man who sired you killed you too.
His wish, his plan, his hand: these murdered you."

And having left such hatred in your house,
will a homecoming really be your dearest wish?
The slightest pretext will suffice for us,
I and your children, to be your enemies,
to welcome you as is appropriate.
By the gods, do not make this my fate,
to be your enemy! And do not be
an enemy to me!

Or sacrifice your child. How will you pray?
Wielding the knife, what prayers can you say—
"Disastrous voyage, bad homecoming too?"
Why on earth should I wish good for you?
If the gods have any judgment, we
cannot treat criminals benevolently.

Say you come home to Argos. And embrace
your children? No; that would be a disgrace.
Fearing that you might kill one of them too,
which of your children will even look at you?
Have you given thought to this at all?
No—you only yearn for power to rule
and lead the army. Here is one just way
to have addressed them: "You want to sail to Troy?
Draw lots, then, to decide whose child must die."
That would be fair, a risk for all to take,
not you alone. Or this: "For Helen's sake
let Menelaus kill Hermione
and keep this trouble in his family."
But no. So now I, your devoted wife,
will lose my child, my child will lose her life,
while Helen keeps her daughter safe and sound,
happy in Sparta. What have I said that's wrong?
If I am right, then you too should be wise,
Agamemnon. Stop the sacrifice!

CHORUS: Be persuaded by your wife, my king.
    To save one's children is a noble thing.

IPHIGENIA: Oh Father, if I had the magic tones
    of Orpheus' music, and could order stones
    to follow me, and could charm everyone,
    if I had that power of persuasion,
    I'd use it now. But only tears are mine,
    and with those tears I'll do the best I can.
    On my knees I beg you: this body—
    you gave it life. Do not take life from me
    so soon, too soon. We love to see the light.
    Do not force me down to the dark gate
    beneath the world. I was the first to say
    "Daddy" to you, and you said "child" to me;
    I was the first one to sit on your knee,
    and you caressed me, and we shared that joy.

Remember? "Little girl," you'd often say,
"shall I see you married happily,
thriving, living a life worthy of me?"
And I would take you by the chin and say,
"What about you, Daddy?
When you are old please come to live with me,
so all your love and care can be repaid."
I can remember every word we said.
But you must have forgotten, now that your desire
is to kill me.
                    By Pelops, your grandfather,
your father Atreus, and my mother here,
do not do this, I beg you!
My mother—she who underwent the pain
of giving birth now suffers it again.
Helen and Paris are lovers, yes, I see,
but what have their affairs to do with me?
Oh, if you are not moved by what I say,
Father, at least then look me in the eye,
give me one kiss to remember you by.

Orestes, baby brother, how can you
help? You can weep along with me.
You can beg our father, as I do,
to spare your sister's life. Young children too
understand when something's ominous.
See, Father? See? His silence has a voice.
Please pay attention to it, and to us.
Do not be shameless, don't be pitiless!
Save my life! Your children—sister, brother—
we touch your beard and beg of you, dear Father:
light is the sweetest thing that we can see.
Below is nothing.
No one in their senses wants to die.
Better live badly than die heroically.
Do not kill me! Don't take my light away!

CHORUS: Helen, what have you done to Agamemnon
and to his children? See—
agony!

AGAMEMNON: Some situations call for pity,
some do not. I understand the distinction.
I'm not devoid of sense.
Also, I love my children. How could you
imagine otherwise? I'm not insane.
It is a dreadful thing I have to do,
equally dreadful if I choose not to.
No, it's not choice. It's obligation.
Do you not see the army's desperation?
The bronze-clad leaders of the Greeks, who all
lust to set sail—
all these heroic men will lack the power
to sail to Troy, lay siege to her proud towers,
unless I make this sacrifice—
so Calchas says.
The army is in love, so great its need
to sail with all possible speed
to the land of the barbarians,
who must not be
allowed to kidnap our wives with impunity!
And think of this: the Greeks at home will slay
my daughters, and you, and you, if I disobey
the goddess's oracle. I am not swayed
by what Menelaus may have said;
I am not influenced by my brother's wish.
My only obligation is to Greece.
Stronger than we, our country gives commands.
Willing, unwilling—it's now out of my hands.
And it depends on you, my child, and me
to keep Greece safe and free.
Barbarians must not steal our wives away!

[*Exit* AGAMEMNON.]

CLYTEMNESTRA: My child, and all you women gathered here,
   you saw him disappear?
   Your father's run away.
   He has deserted you at Hades' door.

IPHIGENIA: Oh Mother, one
   threnody fits us two—
   there will be
   no more light of the sun
   ever, now, for me.

   Oh snowy woods, oh mountaintop
   where Priam left his son!
   He took the baby from its mother
   to be handed over
   to fate, to death—so Paris
   was raised there on Mount Ida.
   You, mountain, you should never
   have sheltered him, saved his life
   so he could grow to manhood
   and become a cowherd
   there by your bright water,
   near the nymphs' bubbling springs,
   near the blossoming meadow.
   Wild grasses there are waving,
   and hyacinths and roses—
   lovely flowers for goddesses to pick.
   And goddesses did come:
   Athena came, and tricky Aphrodite,
   and Hera; Hermes too,
   the messenger of Zeus.
   Cypris' strength was love;
   Athena's was her spear;
   and Hera was the queen
   who shared the bed of Zeus.
   A jealous competition brought them there
   as judges. To judge what?

Beauty. But for me
that contest led to death.
An honor for Greek girls—
but Artemis brought me
as a preliminary
sacrifice for Troy.

Oh Mother, Mother, Mother,
where is my father now?
He has gone away.
He has abandoned me.
Helen—damn her to hell
and damn my evil fate.
I will be slaughtered here
by my unholy father.
Oh Aulis, gathering place,
why did you ever welcome
the bronze-prowed ships
into your harbor here?
I wish that Zeus had never
breathed out and blown a wind—
a different wind, depending:
a wind of joy for some,
for others an ill wind,
a deathly wind for me,
a wind of pain and of necessity.
For some, wind speeds departure;
for some, wind spells delay.

Oh cursed family,
to live a life so short
it seems a single day
under this crushing weight!
Trouble is our tribe's fate.
Think of the agony
Tyndareus' daughter Helen

created for us all,
especially for me.

CHORUS: Dear child, a dreadful thing
has befallen you.
How I wish this story were not true.

IPHIGENIA: Mother, l can see a crowd of men
coming.

CLYTEMNESTRA: And I can see the goddess's son
for whom you came here.

IPHIGENIA: Oh, then let me hide!
Open the doors and let me run inside.

CLYTEMNESTRA: What makes you run away?

IPHIGENIA: Modesty.
I can't look Achilles in the eye.

CLYTEMNESTRA: But why?

IPHIGENIA: This doom-filled marriage shames me. I feel shy.

CLYTEMNESTRA: No modesty, no shame now! Daughter, you
stay here. Be strong. Courage may see us through.

ACHILLES: Oh Leda's daughter, you unfortunate—

CLYTEMNESTRA: You never spoke a truer word than that.

ACHILLES: —the army's shouting terribly.

CLYTEMNESTRA: Yes, and they
are shouting what?

ACHILLES: About your daughter.

CLYTEMNESTRA: What you have just said
   fills me with dread.

ACHILLES: They say that she must die!

CLYTEMNESTRA: Was there no word against this? No outcry?

ACHILLES: I was a target of their anger too.

CLYTEMNESTRA: What now?

ACHILLES: They shouted that they'd stone me.

CLYTEMNESTRA: Because you
   wished to save my daughter?

ACHILLES: Exactly so.

CLYTEMNESTRA: But who would dare to lay a hand on you?

ACHILLES: All the Greeks.

CLYTEMNESTRA: Even the army of the Myrmidons?

ACHILLES: My Myrmidons most of all.

CLYTEMNESTRA: My child, this spells the end for you and me.

ACHILLES: They jeered: my marriage vows were stronger
   than I.

CLYTEMNESTRA: And your reply?

ACHILLES: I begged them not to kill my future bride—

CLYTEMNESTRA: You said the right thing!

ACHILLES: —whose father promised her to me, I said.

CLYTEMNESTRA: Promised her, yes! He sent her here from home.

ACHILLES: Their shouting drowned out what I had to say.

CLYTEMNESTRA: Mobs! I hate and fear them.

ACHILLES: Yes,
but I will be your champion nonetheless.

CLYTEMNESTRA: Against so many? Will you fight alone?

ACHILLES: Look who's coming. Do you see armed men?

CLYTEMNESTRA: Oh, bless your courage—

ACHILLES: I accept your thanks.

CLYTEMNESTRA: —but my daughter:
can she escape slaughter?

ACHILLES: If I can save her, then she will not die.

CLYTEMNESTRA: Will someone come and snatch her violently?

ACHILLES: Odysseus, leading many men this way.

CLYTEMNESTRA: Sisyphus' son?

ACHILLES: That is the man I mean.

CLYTEMNESTRA: Has Odysseus been
sent by the army? Or acting on his own—

ACHILLES: Both. Chosen by the army; willing, too.

CLYTEMNESTRA: —selected as a murderer? What a choice!

ACHILLES: I won't let him get away with this.

CLYTEMNESTRA: Will he seize her and carry her away from here?

ACHILLES: Lady, he'll drag her by her golden hair.

CLYTEMNESTRA: And I—what should I do then?

ACHILLES: Hold on to your daughter. Hold her tight.

CLYTEMNESTRA: I'll clasp her in my arms—I will do that!
    But will that save her?

ACHILLES: We shall see. It may.

IPHIGENIA: Oh Mother, Mother, listen to me now.
    I see you're furious
    at your husband. Mother, what's the use?
    People can endure only so much pain
    and so much fear—no more.
    Yes, it is right
    that we should thank this man
    for his eagerness to help us here.
    But you must see the danger:
    he could enrage the army,
    suffer the worst—and we?
    What would we gain?

    Mother, listen. See,
    these thoughts have come to me.
    I must die.
    I have to die.
    But to die gloriously,

to step free
of lowborn cowardice,
not to be base,
to show no fear—
that is what I wish.
Keep me company,
dear Mother, as I think
this through; and you will see
how right I am.
All Greece now looks to me!
The ships need me
to make their way toward Troy,
to punish the barbarians
for seizing Helen after Paris stole her,
to keep them from abducting
women ever again.
All this I can accomplish
simply by dying! And then my fame
as Greece's liberator
will make people bless my name.
My own dear life—but why
should that mean so much to me?
Thousands of armed men,
countless rowers, sailors, soldiers—
they dare to fight and die
for their insulted country.
And will my clinging to my single life
mean all this cannot be?
How could I justify
the outcome if I refuse to die?
And then consider this:
that Prince Achilles
should not have to do battle
with the whole Greek army,
should not have to die
for just one woman's sake.
Better for one man

to live, to see the light
of day, than countless women!
And think of this:
if it is Artemis' desire that I be sacrificed,
how can I, a mortal woman, hinder
a goddess's deathless will?
That can never be.
Let me bestow this body
on Greece. Oh, sacrifice me
and take Troy!
And let that be how Greece remembers me
for all eternity:
let that victory be
my marriage and my children
and my undying fame.
Greece must rule barbarians
and not the other way.
Barbarians are enslaved;
Greeks are always free.

CHORUS: Young woman, everything you say and do is only noble.
Nevertheless, your god-sent fate is terrible.

ACHILLES: Lady, Agamemnon's daughter: if
god willed it, I would take you as my wife.
I envy Greece: she has you, you have her.
What you have said just now is noble, fair,
and virtuous. From combating heaven, I see
your thoughts have turned to what we need today.

Now that your noble nature is so clear,
I long to be your husband all the more.
If only I could rescue you, take you
home! Let my mother Thetis witness how
it pains me not to brave the whole Greek host
for your sake! Still, remember: death is most
dreadful.

IPHIGENIA: But I say
     no! Helen's beauty has already
     destroyed so many.
     Oh stranger, neither die nor kill for me.
     Let me save my country if I can.

ACHILLES: I have no more to add, then, my lady,
     since to your noble mind things seem this way.
     Your utter excellence no one would deny.
     Nevertheless, should your firm purpose falter,
     listen: I'll leave weapons near the altar.
     I will not let them kill you. I will block
     your murder. When the blade is near your neck
     you may find that you see
     things very differently.
     I will not let you die of foolishness.
     I go now, with my armor, to the place
     of sacrifice. I will be waiting there.

[*Exit* ACHILLES.]

IPHIGENIA: You're weeping, you are wordless, Mother. Why?

CLYTEMNESTRA: Oh god, I have good reason to cry.

IPHIGENIA: Do not make me afraid! Do what I say.

CLYTEMNESTRA: Tell me. I will faithfully obey.

IPHIGENIA: Don't cut your hair. Do not wear black for me.

CLYTEMNESTRA: What are you saying? After you are—gone?

IPHIGENIA: Not gone, not lost. I shall be saved. Your name
     will have, because of me, undying fame.

CLYTEMNESTRA: Am I not allowed to mourn you, then?

IPHIGENIA: No, you are not! And I don't want a grave.

CLYTEMNESTRA: But sacrificial victims always have
    a tomb—

IPHIGENIA: No, Mother. Let my memorial be
    the altar where they will sacrifice me.

CLYTEMNESTRA: What else can I do but listen to you?

IPHIGENIA: Yes—for I am blessed.
    I am the benefactress of all Greece.

CLYTEMNESTRA: And for your sisters—
    what message shall I take back?

IPHIGENIA: Tell them from me not to dress in black.
    No mourning.

CLYTEMNESTRA: Not one loving word from you?

IPHIGENIA: Good-bye from me to them.
    And for Orestes here—
    raise him to be a man.

CLYTEMNESTRA: Kiss him good-bye. You won't see him again.

IPHIGENIA: Little brother, you did what you could
    to help me.

CLYTEMNESTRA: Is there nothing I can do
    back home in Argos, daughter, to help you?

IPHIGENIA: My father and your husband—do not hate
    him.

CLYTEMNESTRA: He must suffer torments for your sake.

IPHIGENIA: Unwillingly,
and on behalf of Greece, he has killed me.

CLYTEMNESTRA: By a vile trick, unworthy of his race.

IPHIGENIA: Who will lead me where
I have to go, before
they come for me and drag me by the hair?

CLYTEMNESTRA: I'll go with you—

IPHIGENIA: Not you, no, no.

CLYTEMNESTRA: —clutching your dress. I will not let you go.

IPHIGENIA: Oh Mother, Mother, I won't weep for you.
Tears have no place here.
Sing with me, girls, to Artemis,
the goddess here at Calchis
where the ships are waiting
to be launched from Aulis—
and all because of me!
Oh my homeland,
Mycenae, mother country—

CHORUS: The citadel of Perseus,
the Cyclopean walls—

IPHIGENIA: you brought me up to be
a light to all of Greece.
I don't regret my death.

CHORUS: Your fame will never die.

IPHIGENIA: Oh sun that lights the day,
I move now to another life,

to a different fate.
Good-bye, beloved light.

CHORUS: Look, see, she moves away,
the victor over Troy,
toward the wreath, the water,
toward the sea.
Blood from her cut throat
will stain the goddess's altar.
The sacrifice is waiting;
the ships are waiting too.
Your father waits for you.
Let us sing a hymn,
as if the news were good.
Oh Artemis, who lusts
for human sacrifice,
speed the Greek army to the town of Troy.
Let Agamemnon crown
his land with victory
and everlasting fame.

[*Exit* IPHIGENIA.]

[*Enter* MESSENGER.]

MESSENGER: Clytemnestra! Lady, do not hide away.
Come outside, hear what I have to say.

CLYTEMNESTRA: I heard you calling me, and I am here—
dazed and suffering and stunned with fear.
Don't you bring news of some catastrophe,
some fresh emergency?

MESSENGER: About your daughter I have news for you—
astounding, awe-inspiring.

CLYTEMNESTRA: Don't delay!
    Tell me right away!

MESSENGER: Dear mistress, I will tell you the whole tale
    from the beginning, unless my powers fail,
    unless the words I use should somehow mix
    the story up—we know the mind plays tricks.

    We'd gotten to the grove of Artemis—
    fragrant flowers and a stand of trees—
    and the whole Greek army
    was mustered there in one assembly,
    one huge gathering.
    And when the king
    saw his daughter moving toward the place—
    the holy grove—set for her sacrifice,
    he groaned and sighed
    and turned his head aside
    and used his cloak
    to wipe his tears. Yes, Agamemnon cried.
    And then his daughter, standing close to him,
    spoke: "Father, see,
    I'm here. I give myself up willingly,
    since that is what my country asks of me.
    Since that is what the prophecies declare,
    I freely dedicate myself to die—now, here.
    Luck to the army! Win the war, and come—
    all of you—victoriously home.
    And let no Greek now touch me. I will not
    require an escort when they cut my throat."

    These were her words. As if deprived of sense,
    awed by her courage and her excellence,
    we all stood waiting. Then Talthybius,
    the army's herald—for this task was his—
    commanded reverent silence

from all of us.
And then Calchas the prophet unsheathed
a knife with a sharp blade
and put it in a holy basket all inlaid
with gold, and placed a garland
on Iphigenia's head.
And then Achilles, Peleus' son—
for he was there—
took the basket and the holy water
and made a circle round the goddess's
altar and spoke: "Oh wild beast slayer, Zeus's daughter,
guider of the pathways of the light
that kindly shines at night,
receive this victim whom we offer you,
virgin blood from a pure source. And may
the Greek fleet sail auspiciously to Troy,
and may the Trojan towers
fall, and may the city
at long last be ours!"

What happened next? Agamemnon and Menelaus
and the whole army—all the rest of us—
gazed at the ground with one communal stare.
Then a priest took a sword and said a prayer
and seemed to be probing the princess's neck
as if he were searching where to strike.
My heart jumped painfully, and I stood numb.
And then the miracle, the wonder, came.
Everyone could clearly hear the blow,
but where was Iphigenia? No one knew.
The priest cried out, and all the soldiers too,
at the unhoped-for vision they now saw—
god-sent, invisible, yet plain as day:
a stately doe lay panting on the ground,
bleeding her life out from a pulsing wound,
drenching the goddess's altar with her blood.
Then Calchas in relief spoke out. He said:

"Captains of the Greek army, turn your eyes
on this providential sacrifice.
This doe that roams the mountains died in place
of Iphigenia, for queenly Artemis!
Welcome this victim. Now there is no need
to stain the altar here with royal blood.
Artemis gladly greets this sacrifice
and grants us a calm voyage, with her grace.
Sailors, now prepare your ships for Troy!
At long last we leave Aulis' sheltered bay
and steer our course toward the Aegean Sea."

Then, once the offering was consumed by fire,
Calchas pronounced a prayer
wishing the army a safe voyage home
after the war.
        My queen, King Agamemnon
has sent me to explain
what the gods have apportioned to his daughter.
Her glory throughout Greece will last forever.
I was there, I saw it—I can say
your daughter toward the gods has flown away.

Do not grieve. And this, my lady—
do not hate King Agamemnon. He
is not your enemy.
What the gods send us none of us can see.
Loving someone, they save them. So today
has seen your daughter live and seen her die.

CHORUS: This mystic message fills me full of joy.
    He says your daughter lives
    among the gods on high.

CLYTEMNESTRA: Oh my daughter, who
    of the gods has stolen you?
    How can I not see,

how can I not say
that these are myths and lies,
tales meant to comfort me?

CHORUS: Look, Lord Agamemnon's coming now.
You'll see he has the same tale to tell you.
The myth is true.

[*Enter* AGAMEMNON.]

AGAMEMNON: Our daughter's destiny is fortunate,
dear wife. Life with the gods is now her fate.
And now the hour to launch the fleet has come,
it's time for you to take our son here home.
Farewell! It may be many years from now,
when I've come home victorious from Troy,
that we'll next speak together, you and I.
Until then, may all be well with you.

CHORUS: Son of Atreus, depart with joy
and then return with joy
once you have taken Troy.

Iphigenia among
the Taurians

CHARACTERS

IPHIGENIA, *daughter of Agamemnon, sister of Orestes*

ORESTES, *son of Agamemnon, brother of Iphigenia*

PYLADES, *Orestes' faithful companion*

CHORUS *of Greek women, attendants of Iphigenia*

HERDSMAN

THOAS, *king of the Taurians*

MESSENGER, *servant of Thoas*

ATHENA, *goddess*

[*Scene*: IPHIGENIA *is standing in front of a large temple on a lonely promontory near the coast.*]

IPHIGENIA: My ancestor Pelops, who was the son
    of Tantalus, coming to Pisa, won
    a race with his swift horses there. Besides
    the race, he won a bride. She was
    the daughter of Oenomaus.
    She gave birth to Atreus, and he
    fathered Agamemnon and Menelaus.
    I am Iphigenia,
    child of Agamemnon
    and of Clytemnestra, his queen,
    who is Tyndareus' daughter.
    And at narrow Aulis, by the water
    of the Euripus
    which when the wind blows
    rakes up the depths of the dark blue sea,
    my father sacrificed me
    to Artemis
    for the sake of Helen. So they say.

    This was where Agamemnon mustered his
    thousand ships, eager to win the prize
    of victory for the Greeks, and punish Troy
    for the outrage when Paris stole away
    the wife of Menelaus, Helen—
    a war of conquest, then;
    also an expedition to pay back
    that insult. But the ships' sails all hung slack;
    the wind was bad for sailing.
    So first my father burned
    sacrificial offerings; then he turned
    to his prophet Calchas, who advised:
    "Oh Agamemnon, who hold high command,
    your ships will never cast off from this land
    until Artemis receives your daughter

as victim at the sacrificial altar.
To that light-bringing goddess once you swore
to offer her the fairest thing of yours that year,
the daughter born to you and to your lady"—
Calchas meant the fairest thing was me—
"so you must sacrifice her."

So it was
they took me from my mother by a ruse
concocted by Odysseus,
pretending I'd be married to Achilles.
When I got there they snatched me, dangled me
over the altar, and the blade was ready,
when—miraculous!—
the goddess Artemis,
intervening, left a doe
on the altar for all the Greeks to see
and spirited me
away to this wild place,
the Taurian land, remote and barbarous.
Barbarians are ruled here by a barbarian,
King Thoas, named for his
speed as a runner. The goddess Artemis
here in her temple has made me a priestess.
And by the ritual customary here,
whose details are too horrible to share,
my sacred task is this: to apprehend
any Greek man
who ventures to this land.
I mark him out as victim, destined for
sacrifice within the precinct here.
The deed I don't perform; others do that.

My dream brought strange visions last night;
let me tell them to the morning light,
if that can help. In sleep it seemed to me
that I had managed to get away

from this place. In Argos, back at home,
I was sleeping in my childhood room.
And as I slept the earth began to quake.
I ran outside and saw the whole house shake;
columns collapsed; it toppled to the ground.
I dreamed one pillar still stood strong and sound.
From its top, blond hair began to grow,
and with a human voice it spoke to me.
Obedient priestess even as I slept,
I poured out a libation, and I wept,
to consecrate this way with holy water
a foreign traveler singled out for slaughter.

What did this dream mean, in the light of day?
Orestes, whom I purified this way,
has died. A house's pillars are its sons.
And every man for whom
I pour libations
I dedicate to doom.
Therefore, even remotely, as a sister
I wish to honor my poor absent brother.
My Greek attendants, King Thoas' gift to me,
will help me to
perform what I must do.
They are not here yet, so I will withdraw
into my home, the goddess's temple, now.

[IPHIGENIA *goes back into the temple.* ORESTES *and* PYLADES *enter cautiously.*]

ORESTES: Look all around. Is anybody near?

PYLADES: I'm scanning here and there and everywhere.

ORESTES: Pylades, could this be the goddess's home,
    the goal for which we've come
    over the sea from Argos?

PYLADES: I think so,
    Orestes. And you should believe it too.

ORESTES: This is the altar where Greek blood is shed?

PYLADES: The top—look here—is stained with something red.

ORESTES: And underneath it, these things hanging are—

PYLADES: —trophies of foreigners who've perished here.
    We must both be vigilant. Take care!

ORESTES: So, Lord Apollo, you've hunted me thus far,
    with your oracles, into this snare.
    Ever since I avenged my father's murder
    by killing my own mother,
    the Furies have pursued me—
    an exile, stained with blood—
    here, there, and everywhere,
    running in circles in an endless race.
    When I asked you, Apollo,
    how I might escape
    this dizzying wheel
    of madness, put an end to my travail,
    find respite from the guilt and fear I feel,
    you told me to come here
    to the land of the Taurians,
    where Artemis, your sister, has an altar.
    And, further, you instructed me to steal
    the goddess's statue out of here—it fell,
    they say, into the temple from the sky—
    to take this statue, either on the sly,
    by some clever trick,
    or simply by good luck.
    And then, when I had done this perilous feat,
    to transport it to Athens would complete
    my task—then there would be

no more for me
to do. I would be cured of all my pain,
the suffering and exhaustion I have borne.
And I believed your words, so I have come,
a stranger, to a place
that seems unkind to strangers.

So, Pylades, let me know—
you share this burden equally with me—
what shall we do now?
High walls are all around us. How to climb?
If we put ladders up, we shall be seen.
Or pry these bronze doors open, boldly enter?
If we are caught, death will be swift and sure.
Here is what I think: rather than die,
let's take our ship and simply sail away.

PYLADES: We must not and we will not run away.
Let's heed the god, whatever he may say.
We'll leave this place now, find some cave to hide,
splashed by the dark sea, and go inside,
far from our ship. Should anybody see
the ship, the king would learn, and you and I
would be taken into custody.
But soon as cloaking night comes, we must dare
to get that gleaming statue out of there
by any means we manage, foul or fair.
Good men brave pain and danger; cowards do not.
We haven't sailed so far to find this spot
only to turn back now and run away.

ORESTES: Well said, Pylades. You've persuaded me.
For now, we have to find a place to hide.
Let me not be the reason for the word
of the oracle to go unfulfilled.
You have said it exactly: *we must dare*
to undertake this deed, young as we are.

[ORESTES *and* PYLADES *leave.* IPHIGENIA *and the* CHORUS *of Greek women who attend her at the temple enter.*]

CHORUS: You who live by the grinding clash
    of rocks that smash
    together in this sea
    to strangers so unfriendly,
    keep holy silence.
    No sound at all.
    Be still.
    Mountain goddess, daughter of Leto,
    barefoot I pace
    in this holy place
    toward your beautiful pillared
    gold-roofed court.
    I attend the one
    who keeps the keys to the temple.
    I left behind
    Greece, her towers and her walls,
    her green woods, her running horses.
    I left behind
    Europe, my ancestral home.
    Here I am, lady. What is it now?
    What worries you?
    Daughter of the man
    with a thousand ships under his command
    and ten thousand soldiers too,
    of the man who took and toppled
    the towers and walls of Troy,
    oh eldest child of Atreus' son,
    what is it?
    What can we do?

IPHIGENIA: Women, I am tangled
    in a web of lamentation.
    The Muses do not grace

elegies like this—
no lyre, no melody,
only mourning for a fallen house.
Catastrophe
has come upon me.
I am weeping for my brother.
This was my dream vision
last night. Now it is dawn.
Oh god, my father's line
is utterly erased.
I have no family.
Oh cursed Argos,
an evil fate
stole my only brother
and sent him down to Hades.
And so l hold this bowl
in which to mix libations for the dead
and pour them down onto
the surface of the earth:
fresh milk from mountain cows;
Bacchus' wine; golden honey;
I mix these, pour them out
to soothe the dead.
Give me the golden cup there
for the death libation.

Oh son of Agamemnon underground,
I send these offerings down
to you as if you're dead.
Take, accept, receive them.
I cannot cut my hair,
I cannot leave a blond
strand upon your tomb.
I cannot weep for you.
Far from our fatherland,
far from our childhood home,

this is where I live:
this place where they believe
I'm lying dead and buried.

CHORUS: Lady, I'll chant a song for you,
nothing like the Asian tunes—
no yell of triumph, but a dirge
for the dead down in Hades' house.
The light of the house of Atreus,
my fatherland, my ancestral home,
oh god, has guttered and gone out.
The kings of Argos were lucky once,
but luck was followed by disaster,
trouble piled on trouble, as,
revolving with his winged horses,
the sun god swung across the sky.
That golden lamb brought pain and woe,
grief and death. Tantalus' children
punish the house for ancient crimes.
We cannot change fate's dark designs.

IPHIGENIA: From the start I was unlucky.
From my mother's marriage bed
the Fates of sorrow spun for me
a web of anguish, a net of pain.
Greek heroes wanted me for their own,
wooed me—me, the eldest child
of the unfortunate daughter of Leda.
My mother had no better luck,
since she bore me and brought me up
to be a sacrificial victim.
Where is the glory and joy in that?
In a horse-drawn chariot
they brought me there
to the sandy shore
of Aulis, as a bride for the son

of the Nereid Thetis—oh god, a bride
for Lord Achilles.

And my life now?
I live in this house on the shore of a sea
called the Unfriendly to Strangers Sea.
I am a stranger in my life.
I have no husband, I have no children,
I have no friends, I have no city.
I do not celebrate
Hera of Argos
or weave an image
of Athena
and the Titans
on my loom
in many colors.
No craft, no music:
my task is to spill
upon these altars
the blood of strangers—
no lyre, no song
except their cry
of agony, except the tears
of their despair.
Even all these
I have forgotten.
I weep for the one
back home in Argos,
my brother, still a nursing baby
when I left him, a tiny child
cradled in his mother's arms,
Argos' lawful king, Orestes.

CHORUS: Look! Here comes a herdsman from the seashore.
He must have news for you.

[*Enter* HERDSMAN.]

HERDSMAN: Lady,
    this is a strange tale I'm about to tell.

IPHIGENIA: Why,
    what is strange? Say what you have to say.

HERDSMAN: Escaping the dark Symplegades,
    two young men have just reached these
    shores—a double sacrifice
    to the goddess Artemis.
    Get everything in readiness—
    lustral water, barley too—
    for the deed you now must do.

IPHIGENIA: Where have they come from? Can the clothes they wear
    tell us?

HERDSMAN: I know they're Greeks, but nothing more.

IPHIGENIA: Did you hear them speak to one another
    by name?

HERDSMAN: Pylades, one of them called the other.

IPHIGENIA: And did Pylades' friend have a name too?

HERDSMAN: He must, but no one heard him spoken to.

IPHIGENIA: And where were these men captured?

HERDSMAN: On the shore
    of the Unfriendly to Strangers Sea.

IPHIGENIA: Why were you there,
    you, a cattle herder?

HERDSMAN: Because we
    wash our cattle in the salty sea.

IPHIGENIA: Tell me again
    where and how you captured them;
    I want to know.
    The goddess's altar
    has never yet
    with the blood of Greeks been wet.

HERDSMAN: Our oxen that graze in the woodlands—we
    were just about to wash them in the sea
    that flows through the Symplegades, whose waves
    have worn away the rocks and formed a cave
    where fishermen take shelter. One of our
    herdsmen, spying two young men in there,
    ran back to us on tiptoe, crying: "See!
    Some kind of gods sit up there!" Reverently
    another of us raised his hands in prayer:
    "Palaimon, Leukothea's son, you who care
    for ships, have mercy on us! Or perhaps you are
    the Dioscuri who sit upon this shore,
    or Nereus' children and the Nereids' sires?"
    Another of us laughed and mocked these prayers
    and said the men were shipwrecked sailors there,
    hiding, who knew our laws and were in fear
    for their lives, lest they be sacrificed.
    Since what he said made sense to most of us,
    we resolved to hunt the strangers down,
    as is customary in this land.
    One of the men now got up from the stone
    where they had crouched. His head shook up and down,
    he groaned, his hands were trembling, he seemed mad.
    "You see that bitch, Pylades? She's dog-eyed!
    And here, this snake from hell
    is set to kill
    me with her poisonous brood—

and this one here
breathing out fire and blood
flaps her wings and clasps
my mother in her grasp—
my mother, petrified, a block of stone
to hurl at me,
to kill me!
Where can I go?
Where can I run?"
But there were no monsters,
only the low-
ing cattle, and the dogs were barking too.
There were no other sounds at all to hear,
no noises near.
He only thought he heard the Furies there.

We stood in silence. Was he going to die?
Oh no. With sword unsheathed, he rushed upon
our herd of oxen fiercely as a lion
and stabbed their flanks and gored their sides—for these
oxen to his sick mind were the Erinyes.
A flower blooming blood,
the salty sea turned red.
And when we saw such slaughter being done,
first everybody armed themselves, and then
we blew conch shells to summon aid. We thought
that we could never match them in a fight,
two such strong young men.
Soon a crowd had gathered. But we saw
the stranger now
no longer seemed mad.
His mouth dripped foam
and he fell down.
We saw this and drew near
to strike him. But the other foreigner
wiped his friend's face clean

of foam, guarded his body, shielded him
with his thick cloak
and fended off whatever blows we struck,
caring for his companion lovingly.
Sane now again, and back
on his feet,
seeing that we continued to attack,
the stranger groaned aloud. But we came
on steadily, pelting both of them with stones.
This was the moment when we heard him say
"Pylades, now we'll die—but gloriously.
Take your sword in your hand, and follow me!"
They waved their swords at us; we ran away,
crowding the stony pathways—although some,
who stood their ground, went right on pelting them.
Though driven off, our men came strongly back
with yet more stones, renewing the attack.
But not a single pebble that we threw
so much as grazed the sacred victims—they
had divine protection. When we won,
it was sheer numbers, not our bravery.
We circled them and knocked their swords away
with stones as weapons. This
was no victorious rout—
they were simply tired out.
They knelt exhausted on the ground.
We took them to the high command,
our king, who saw them, sent them on to you
for sacrifice. You know what you must do.

Such fine young foreigners—
are they not the answer to your prayers,
lady? If you kill these men,
Greece will be punished in return
for your murder. Greece will pay
your sacrifice's penalty.

CHORUS: Strange story of these men who have appeared
    from Greece, washed up on our unfriendly shore.

IPHIGENIA: Go bring them, the two strangers, both here now.
    I know what must be done to them, and how.

[*Exit* HERDSMAN.]

My heart is all one throbbing scar.
I could be gentle and kind before
when face to face with foreigners;
could weep for my Greek prisoners.
But last night's dream has hardened me.
Orestes is dead, he cannot see
the light of the sun—
such was my vision.
It's made me hate all those who come.
We who have suffered a harsh fate
are not fond of the fortunate:
this truth I deeply understand.
But no wind has blown toward this land—
no breeze from Zeus, not a single breath—
Helen, whose folly caused my death,
and Menelaus. Had they come,
I would have had retribution
and planned another Aulis here
to match the crime that was done there
when the Greeks seized me, held me high,
just like a calf about to die,
and slaughtered me. Who took the lead
in this? My father. My flesh and blood.

Oh god, the scene is burned into my brain:
how I reached out to touch my father's chin
and how I clasped his knees and clung to him:
"Oh Father, you are marrying me to shame!
The house is full of wedding music now,

my mother sings, her women sing—but you
are killing me. My promised bridegroom is
not the son of Peleus, Achilles,
no. In a chariot of deceit
you drove me here to wed in blood.
My bridegroom is death.
My altar is my tomb."
I was ashamed; I hid my face
behind my veil; did not embrace
my little brother, who now is
down in death's dark house.
I did not kiss my sister good-bye.
I was modest, I was shy;
I who was about to be
a bride, about to go to the house
of my bridegroom Achilles.
I thought there would be ample time
to exchange loving greetings with my family
when I came back to Argos,
when I came home.

Artemis' laws, her sophistry—
these make no sense to me.
Whoever has touched blood,
childbirth, or death—that person is taboo,
must not pollute the altars, no no no,
must stay
far away.
Yet for this very same divinity
her pleasure, her great joy
is sacrifice,
is spilling human blood.
How could Zeus's lover
Leto, who gave birth to Artemis,
breed a goddess ignorant as this?
Another thing I find hard to believe:
that the gods at Tantalus' feast

smacked their lips and savored his son's flesh.
I will not swallow this.
So too the people here—
people who love to kill—
blame their lust to spill
their fellow creatures' blood,
blame this savagery, on a god.
I will not believe this.
I am incredulous.
No gods are that bad.

CHORUS: Dark paths cut through
the sea's black blue.
The maddened gadfly flew away
to what is called the Unfriendly Sea,
exchanging Europe for Asia.
Who on earth can the people be
who left behind the marshy reeds
of the Eurotas, and the stream
of Dirce, to come here instead
to this untamed land, a country
where to honor Zeus's daughter
human blood drops from the altar?
Did they row
over the sea?
Did breezes swell
the linen sails
of their chariot, their ship?
Were they following the trail
of riches? Hope, a cherished friend,
still brings trouble to mankind.
For wealth-crazed men who cross the sea
to foreign cities, one fantasy
drives them on insatiably.
The vision of riches never came
to fruition for some of them:
it was too soon or else too late.

Fortunate are the moderate.
The Symplegades—did they steer through these
or the shores of Phineus
raked by wind? Did they skim along
the waves near Amphitrite's home
where Nereus' fifty daughters sit
in a circle and sing their song?
Did a south wind swell
their bellying sail
or with a west wind did they steer
toward the shore
where flocks of seabirds forever nest?
On this white island eternally
Achilles runs races beside the sea,
along the shores of the Unfriendly to Strangers Sea.

If only what my lady prays
ardently for would come to pass—
if Leda's dear daughter, leaving Troy,
would only turn her steps this way.
Then every hair of Helen's head
with crimson dew would soon be red.
Dead by my lady's hand, Helen would
pay back the penalty of blood.
But even sweeter, oh my god,
would be if some sailor came
from Greece, came here and set me free
from the shackles of slavery.
May I, if only in a dream,
sing to my country and my home
songs of victory and joy,
songs of shared prosperity.

[ORESTES and PYLADES, *guarded, enter.*]

But look—two men
are coming near,

hands tied together
with bonds they share.
Fresh sacrifice
for the goddess here!
Hush. Keep still.
A gift from Greece
walks toward the temple
of this place.
What the herdsman said is true.
Take them, lady, if they please you,
the victims your city celebrates
but our own law abominates:
holy here, a horror there.

IPHIGENIA: So. My first care
is to safeguard the goddess's property.
Untie these strangers' hands; let them go free,
for they are holy victims. Then go in;
make preparations for what must be done.

[*Attendants unshackle* ORESTES *and* PYLADES *and go into the temple, leaving the two men with* IPHIGENIA.]

You poor young men,
who was your mother? Who was your father?
And if you had a sister,
then she too
will be bereft of you—
of both of you.
Who can foresee, who knows,
the paths that fate may choose?
What the gods send is murky and obscure.
Where trouble first arose,
and how, is never clear;
nor is it ever clear
where things may go from here.
Chance leads us into dense confusion.

Miserable strangers, where have you come from?
You must have voyaged far across the sea;
and even lengthier will be your stay
away from home eternally
in the world below.

ORESTES: Woman, whoever you may be, why moan,
grieving for troubles that are ours alone?
If you plan
to kill someone,
it makes no sense to try
to ease their dread of death with sympathy.
And why, when close to death, when no escape
is possible, should anybody weep?
Scorned as a fool yet dying just the same,
he doubles all the trouble he is in.
What will be, will be. So let it be.
And do not weep for us. We clearly see
and understand the custom of this place.
We know that we will be a sacrifice.

IPHIGENIA: Which of you is Pylades? That is my
first question.

ORESTES: He is—if that gives you any joy.

IPHIGENIA: And which Greek city is
home to Pylades?

ORESTES: Why ask us?
How does it benefit you to know this?

IPHIGENIA: Did one mother give birth to you two?

ORESTES: We're bound by ties of love, not family.

IPHIGENIA: The name your father gave you—what
is it?

ORESTES: "Unlucky" would have been appropriate.

IPHIGENIA: I ask your name, but you describe your fate.

ORESTES: You'll sacrifice my body, not my name.

IPHIGENIA: All the same,
why not tell me? Why
are you so reluctant,
so grudging, so haughty?

ORESTES: If I die nameless, no one can laugh at me.

IPHIGENIA: So you will not even name your city?

ORESTES: What good would that do me?
I am about to die.

IPHIGENIA: But as a favor to me? Tell me, please.

ORESTES: Glorious Argos—that's where I was raised.

IPHIGENIA: Oh god—can there be truth in that claim?

ORESTES: Mycenae, wealthy once—that was my home.

IPHIGENIA: Oh, your arrival here was longed for so!

ORESTES: I never longed to come here. Maybe you
for some reason longed for me to come.

IPHIGENIA: So were you exiled from your native land?

ORESTES: Yes. No. It's hard to understand.
I did choose exile. Also I did not.

IPHIGENIA: Could you tell me something that
     I long to hear?

ORESTES: It adds no weight to what I have to bear,
     so yes.

IPHIGENIA: It is this:
     have you ever heard of Troy?
     The legend of that place is everywhere.

ORESTES: I'd give a lot not to know that nightmare.

IPHIGENIA: Has Troy been conquered? That is what I hear.

ORESTES: The stories that you hear are not a lie.

IPHIGENIA: And Helen—tell me, has she come back home
     to Menelaus?

ORESTES: She has. And it was evil, this return.
     It harmed a person dear to me.

IPHIGENIA: Where is Helen now?
     She owes something to me
     for an old injustice,
     an injury.

ORESTES: She lives in Sparta now just as before,
     with her husband.

IPHIGENIA: Curse the wicked whore!
     All Greece hates Helen. I am not alone.

ORESTES: No, you are far from the only one.
     Helen's marriage also affected me.

IPHIGENIA: And have the Greeks returned, as people say,
    from Troy?

ORESTES: You are interrogating me.
    Too many questions packed too close together.

IPHIGENIA: I need to know the answers! I
    must learn the truth before you die.

ORESTES: Go on, since you desire it. I will try.

IPHIGENIA: A man named Calchas—did he come
    home from Troy, did he return?
    They say he was a prophet.

ORESTES: And they say
    he's dead. That was the rumor in Mycenae.

IPHIGENIA: Thanks, blessed goddess! And Laertes' son?

ORESTES: Still alive. Still far from home.

IPHIGENIA: Good. Damn him—may he die
    far away
    from his home in Ithaka.

ORESTES: There is no need to curse Odysseus.
    His life's a wreck already.

IPHIGENIA: And Thetis
    the Nereid's son Achilles—what of him?

ORESTES: Dead. In Aulis he was a bridegroom;
    that marriage never came to anything.

IPHIGENIA: Marriage? False marriage, as they all can say
    who suffered through it.

ORESTES: But, lady, who are you?
On all things Greek you question me
with so much knowledge, and so cleverly.

IPHIGENIA: Greece is my native country. But when I
was still a child, they—I was taken away.

ORESTES: Your thirst for news from Greece, then—now I see.

IPHIGENIA: What of that general, the man they say
is fortunate and blessed?

ORESTES: I do not know
of any generals I would call blessed.

IPHIGENIA: Lord Agamemnon, son of Atreus—
that was his name.

ORESTES: I tell you I don't know!
This is not a subject to pursue.

IPHIGENIA: Please tell me, stranger, for the love of god.
Do me that favor.

ORESTES: The poor man has died,
and in his death he has destroyed another.

IPHIGENIA: Died? What disaster—
how did he come to die?

ORESTES: Why are you weeping? What was he to you?

IPHIGENIA: I'm mourning for his lost prosperity.

ORESTES: Murdered by his wife—an awful death.

IPHIGENIA: I mourn for murderer and murdered both.

ORESTES: Then stop right there and do not ask me more!

IPHIGENIA: One more question: does she still draw breath,
    this wife who killed her husband?

ORESTES: No. Her son
    killed her in retribution.

IPHIGENIA: House shaken to its foundations, family
    shattered and ruined! Why
    would any son commit an act like this?

ORESTES: Because
    of his father's murder. This was justice.

IPHIGENIA: I pity him. So
    the son's crime was a just one—virtuous too.

ORESTES: A just crime? Maybe.
    The gods saw matters differently.

IPHIGENIA: Were other children left besides the son?

ORESTES: A girl, Electra—the unmarried one.

IPHIGENIA: And of the daughter who
    was sacrificed—what do
    they say?

ORESTES: Only that she
    can no longer see
    the light. They say
    that she is dead and gone.

IPHIGENIA: Wretched girl and wretched father, then,
    who killed his daughter—

ORESTES: Yes, the daughter who
   was put to death for Helen's sake—
   woman and reason each bad as the other.

IPHIGENIA: And that daughter's brother,
   son of the murdered father—
   is he in Argos still? Is he alive?

ORESTES: If to be alive
   is to live
   everywhere and nowhere, he's alive.

IPHIGENIA: Good-bye, false dreams, good-bye.
   I see now that you lie.

ORESTES: The gods are wise, they say.
   Yet the gods see
   no more of truth than dreams that flutter by.
   Between the mortal world and the divine,
   confusion reigns. A careful man believes
   a prophecy, yet still he comes to grief.

CHORUS: And we have questions! Who can tell
   whether our mothers and fathers still
   live and breathe on Earth?
   Who knows?
   Who can tell?

IPHIGENIA: Listen! A plan has flashed into my mind
   to help you and myself at the same time.
   Surely the perfect outcome always is
   gain for everyone; for no one, loss.
   So if I spare your life, would you
   do this for me: would you go
   to Argos, where my loved ones live, and take
   them a message for my sake?
   Take them a tablet that would say

my captive wrote it, one who pitied me
because he understood my hand was not
what killed him; rather, custom's heavy weight,
since to the goddess that
death was what seemed right.
No one I knew,
even if I spared his life, could make his way
to Argos, to my home and family.
But you—
you know Mycenae, know the people there,
know those whom I hold dear,
and you seem kind, you do not seem to be
angry at me,
so go! And your reward will not be slight:
one little letter bears your whole life's weight.
But since the city's law ordains it so,
let your companion be
parted from you
and be the goddess's victim in your place.

ORESTES: I like what you have said. I disagree
with just one thing: to kill this man would be
a crushing blow to me.
Mine is the cargo of catastrophe;
he generously sails along with me,
sharing the burden of my troubles. So
I cannot in good conscience help you
if my doing that should spell his end.
No; do this. Give my friend
the tablet. Let him go
with it to Argos; that way he helps you.
If there is someone who
wishes here to sacrifice me—do.
It is vile
to hurl your friends into disaster while
yourself escaping, getting off scot-free.

This man happens to be dear to me,
and I want him to see the light of day
no less than I.

IPHIGENIA: You noble spirit! Anyone can see
how good you are, how strong your loyalty
to those who have shown loyalty to you.
If anyone from my own family
still survives, then this is what I pray:
that he may be
just such a man as you!
Strangers, I want both of you to know:
I have a brother. But he's far away,
too far for me to feast my eyes on him.
So. Let me send this man,
since that is your desire,
on with the tablet, and you will die here.
That is what you seem to ask of me.

ORESTES: I have a question: who
dares to perform the act of sacrifice?

IPHIGENIA: I do.
Such is my service to the goddess here.

ORESTES: No one would envy you. No one would aspire
to do this vile
deed of ill omen.

IPHIGENIA: That may be.
I am forced to it by necessity.

ORESTES: So you, a woman, can
take up a sword, use it to kill a man?

IPHIGENIA: I pour the lustral water on your head.

ORESTES: Who is it, then, whose blade will strike me dead,
    if I may ask?

IPHIGENIA: Inside the temple there
    are people with the expertise to care
    for that part of the ritual.

ORESTES: And my tomb?
    What of my burial, once the deed is done?

IPHIGENIA: A sacred flame is burning in that cave,
    there where the rocks split.

ORESTES: Gods, if I could have
    my sister's be the hands that tend me when
    I am a body only.

IPHIGENIA: You poor man, whoever you may be,
    that wish will not come true.
    As for your sister, she is far away
    from this savage place.
    But since it happens you have come from Argos,
    I myself will do everything I can.
    I will omit no honor:
    I'll deck your grave with treasure,
    pour on golden olive oil, add wine
    for a libation
    to quench the embers. Then
    onto your burned-out pyre
    I will slowly pour
    dark honey from bees
    that swarm along the mountainside.
    All this I will do when you are dead.

    Now I'll go in and bring the tablet out
    from the temple. And let me not

be called cruel to these prisoners. Do guard
them, yes, but let their hands remain untied.
And, oh,
maybe, maybe
the news I will send home
to Argos, to the one
most dear to me,
will bring him unimaginable joy,
unhoped-for joy. He thought that I
was dead, but no—
I am alive, I breathe.
For him to learn this will be joy, will be
pleasure beyond belief.

[IPHIGENIA *goes into the temple.*]

CHORUS: Poor man, I weep for you.
    Your blood will flow
    into the sacrificial basin—

ORESTES: No
    need for lamentations. Farewell!

CHORUS: But you, young man, on whom the Fates still smile—
    you will travel home. We honor you.

PYLADES: Why honor me?
    When a man's dear friends die,
    there is no honor, there's no need for envy.

CHORUS: This is a cruel ceremony. Who
    is in a worse position,
    a more desperate situation,
    who's more to be pitied—he or he?
    My mind wings back and forth and to and fro:
    should I weep first for you? Or for you?

ORESTES: My god. Pylades, do
  you feel what I feel now?

PYLADES: I do not know.
  I can't say. You ask me.

ORESTES: This young woman here—just who is she?
  So Greek, her questions! And she somehow knew
  about the war at Troy;
  about the Greeks' homecoming too;
  Calchas the prophet's and Achilles' name,
  and Agamemnon's miserable fame—
  she expressed pity for his tragic life,
  she asked about his children and his wife.
  She cannot be from here. Her native land
  has to be Argos. Why else would she send a
  letter there, and why else would she be
  as anxious for Argive prosperity
  as if it were her own?

PYLADES: To all you say,
  yes! You said it first, and I agree.
  Although there's just one thing:
  everyone learns the sufferings of a king.
  Royal misfortunes are widely known
  to those who pay attention.
                          But listen: I
  have thought of something else.

ORESTES: Tell it to me!
  Thoughts shaped into words—these we can see.

PYLADES: If you die, for me to see the sun
  would be a disgrace, an utter shame.
  When you sailed here, I came
  as your companion, so let me die
  as your companion too.

If I survive you, then I will be known
in Argos and in Phocis, all around,
as a wretched coward. It will seem
to many that I hatched an evil scheme—
for their own thoughts are evil—to sail home,
having deserted you, left you alone
with your affairs in chaos. And what then?
This: that I plotted to usurp your place
by marrying your sister. What disgrace!
Just to imagine this fills me with fear.
Better by far that I die with you here,
be sacrificed beside you, share your pyre,
famed as your friend, your faithful friend forever,
not your deserter,
not your destroyer.

ORESTES: Be still, and let me bear this weight alone.
I won't take two griefs; I can shoulder one.
What you have called a painful source of blame
for yourself—would I not feel the same
if to my shame
I allowed you to die?
Considering how the gods have dealt with me,
to lose my life is no great price to pay.
But you are prosperous, lucky, undefiled.
Ill-fated, godless, I'm misfortune's child
without a home
to call my own.
You have a future and an ancestry.

Should you survive, you could have children too
with my sister, whom I gave to you;
you could live out a blessed life in joy.
My name would be preserved; our family
would not descend into obscurity,
childlessness, invisibility,
and vanish as if it had never been.

You must go home
and live the life to which you are the heir.
But first, give me your right hand—put it here—
and promise me, when you get home to Greece
and to the meadows horses love, in Argos,
that you'll erect a burial mound there
with a memorial for me.
And let my sister pour
her tears into this tomb, and cut her hair.
Proclaim my death to everyone—my slaughter:
how I died at the altar
purified, a holy sacrifice,
dead at the Argive woman's hands.
Do not desert my sister.
Not she alone
but our ancestral home
is in need of you.

And now farewell, my dearest friend. Good-bye.
You used to hunt with me;
we grew up together, side by side.
You shared the burden of the heavy load
fate has assigned to me.

A prophet who deceived with prophecy,
Phoebus Apollo lied to us.
He drove me far from home,
in flight from my dear country, in my fear
and shame at what he'd prophesied before.
I was obedient to him—I slew
my mother. And now I am dying too.

PYLADES: You'll have your tomb. And I will not betray
your sister's bed. Poor friend, I'll love you more
dead than living. And yet—here you are,
untouched still by the oracle, although
you did come close to death. You are close now.

But there's a pattern that we sometimes see:
change can be nourished by extremity.

ORESTES: Enough of this. The god's words are no use.
Here comes the woman now, out of her house.

[*Enter* IPHIGENIA, *carrying a tablet.*]

IPHIGENIA: You—go inside. Get all in readiness.
Help those who prepare the sacrifice.
This letter—I'm entrusting it to you,
strangers. Now hear what else you both can do.
People in trouble do not have a prayer
of calm once they have left behind despair
and turned toward hope. So this is what I fear:
that you, once you have sailed away from here,
will forget about me, will ignore
my heart's desire.

ORESTES: What is it that you want? What can I say
to calm this new anxiety?

IPHIGENIA: First let him reach my native land.
Then let him swear
that once he's there
he will hand
this letter to my loved ones,
and to them alone.

ORESTES: And in exchange what will your promise be?

IPHIGENIA: To do or not do what? Explain to me.

ORESTES: To let him leave this savage place alive.

IPHIGENIA: How could he do this errand otherwise?

ORESTES: And to all this will the king agree?

IPHIGENIA: Yes. And to speed your friend upon his way,
I will be there.

ORESTES: Good. Swear.
You tell him what to say.

IPHIGENIA: Say you will hand this to those dear to me.

PYLADES: I'll hand this letter to those dear to you.

IPHIGENIA: And I'll conduct you safely past the Blue
Black Boulders—

PYLADES: And which god will you
call to witness as I swear to this?

IPHIGENIA: Her whose temple this is: Artemis.

PYLADES: And I call Zeus to witness,
lord of the gods, the great king of the sky—

IPHIGENIA: And if you break your word? If you betray me?

PYLADES: Then may I never reach home! What of you?
If you break your word, what price will you pay?

IPHIGENIA: Never to set foot in my native land.
Never to see Argos, my home, again.

PYLADES: Listen. There's something we are leaving out.

IPHIGENIA: If it is worth considering, tell me what.

PYLADES: There should be this condition: if the ship
should sink, her cargo all be swallowed up

together with this letter, but if I
survive—this oath will no longer bind me.

IPHIGENIA: It's better if we have a backup plan.
So let me do this, then:
all that is written here I'll say to you
and you in turn can pass it on
to those dear to me.
That way we cannot fail.
If all goes well,
the letter will arrive
and will speak silently;
but even if the letter's lost at sea,
so long as you survive, you rescue me.

PYLADES: What you suggest works well both for me and you.
So tell me who,
when I'm in Argos, I should hand this to—
and tell me too
exactly what I should report from you.

IPHIGENIA: Tell Orestes, Agamemnon's son—

PYLADES: Oh god!

IPHIGENIA: Why do you call on god's name? I'm not done.

PYLADES: It was a slip. It means nothing. Go on.

IPHIGENIA: "Orestes"—I will say it one more time;
do not forget that name!—
"here is what Iphigenia
has to say to you,
Iphigenia who, sacrificed at Aulis, did not die,
though that is what they say—"

ORESTES: Where is she? Dead—brought back to life once more?

IPHIGENIA: Stop interrupting me. You see her here.
    "Brother, do this for me before you die:
    bring me home to Argos! Rescue me
    from this place of cruel savagery
    where slaughtering strangers, strangely, is what I
    find myself bound to do—"

ORESTES: Pylades,
    what should I say?
    Where on earth are we? What is this place?

IPHIGENIA: "—or else I'll put a curse upon your house."
    If he does not believe you
    when you say all this,
    then tell him how the goddess Artemis
    saved me. She put a doe
    in my place on the altar.
    My father, thinking this deer was his daughter,
    plunged in his sword and killed—not me, the deer.
    Artemis brought me here
    to live.
           So much the letter says; and you
    are ready to report its contents now.

PYLADES: This promise is an easy one for me
    to keep, my lady, and the same is true
    for what you've sworn. So now without delay
    let me fulfill it. See:
    here is the letter that I hand you now,
    Orestes, from your sister Iphigenia,
    according to our vow.

ORESTES: And I accept it, I receive it—not
    to read, not yet, no, to enjoy the sweet
    taste not of written words but what is real.
    Sister! I hardly know yet how to feel,

but let me try
half incredulously
to put my arms around you
and dare to hope this wonder can be true.

[ORESTES *tries to embrace* IPHIGENIA.]

IPHIGENIA: Stranger, keep away!
    I am the goddess's servant
    and your hands defile
    my sacred clothing. To touch me is vile,
    is blasphemy.

ORESTES: My sister, you and I
    were sired by the same man.
    So, child of Agamemnon,
    do not spurn me, do not turn from me,
    the brother whom you thought you'd never see.

IPHIGENIA: My brother—you? No, this is foolishness.
    My brother is in Nauplion or Argos
    or some such place,
    lost, lost.

ORESTES: No, no, poor woman. He's not there; he's here.

IPHIGENIA: Does this mean Clytemnestra,
    Tyndareus's daughter—
    was she your mother?

ORESTES: Yes, and Pelops' grandson was my father.

IPHIGENIA: Do you have any proof of what you say?

ORESTES: I have. But wait—first ask me
    something, anything, about the place

we both were raised in. Ask me
about the palace—our ancestral house.

IPHIGENIA: No, speak and let me listen.

ORESTES: I'll tell you
the story that Electra told to me—
our sister Electra. Have you heard
of the bad blood
between Atreus and Thyestes—that old feud?

IPHIGENIA: Something about a golden lamb, I know—
some quarrel?

ORESTES: Yes! And you
wove that legend on your loom, remember?

IPHIGENIA: Oh my dear,
you wake old memories, you come so near—

ORESTES: You also wove the story of the sun
and how it changed its heavenly path.

IPHIGENIA: That one
I also wove—now it comes back to me—
worked it into my artful tapestry.

ORESTES: The bath our mother gave you to prepare
you for Aulis and your wedding there—
do you remember this?

IPHIGENIA: Oh yes.
That memory nothing can take away—
the noble marriage that awaited me.

ORESTES: And this as well: you sent a lock of hair
back to our mother as a keepsake?

IPHIGENIA: Yes,
    a token for my tomb, my memory—
    all I could send was that small piece of me.
    My body was elsewhere.

ORESTES: And here's the proof of everything I say:
    the ancient spear
    belonging to Pelops, our ancestor—
    that spear with which he vanquished Oenomaus
    and took Hippodameia as his bride—
    that very spear they hid
    in our house, inside
    the bedroom where you slept when you were small.
    I saw it all.

IPHIGENIA: You are nothing else than dear to me,
    dearer than dear. Let me
    hold you. Here you are,
    Orestes, oh my brother. You are far
    from Argos—you are here.

ORESTES: And you are here! I thought that you were dead.
    Now I can clasp you in my arms instead.

IPHIGENIA: I moan, I sob, I cry.
    My eyes are wet with joy.

ORESTES: My tears are flowing too.
    I weep along with you.

IPHIGENIA: You were a baby when I went away—
    an infant dandled in a nurse's arms
    in our ancestral house.

ORESTES: Oh, this is joy,
    this great good fortune, more than I can say.

IPHIGENIA: And what can I say? Only this: my soul,
  before this miracle
  words falter and are still.

ORESTES: From now until
  the end may we be fortunate together.

IPHIGENIA: Friends, this joy, this pleasure
  is so new to me
  I fear it will grow wings and fly
  out of my hands into the sky.
  Our house, our hearth, our home, our native land,
  Cyclopean walls, Mycenae,
  you all are dear to me.
  To all of you I give
  thanks that my brother here is still alive,
  that you raised and nourished him to be
  a light to our domain and to our family.

ORESTES: In family we may be fortunate,
  my sister—but less blessed in the fate
  life has bestowed on both of us.

IPHIGENIA: How can I forget
  the knife held to my throat
  by our father with his mind awry?

ORESTES: I was not there, but I can see,
  I can envision it in my mind's eye.

IPHIGENIA: Brother, they sang no wedding hymn for me
  when I was led
  to the false marriage bed
  of Achilles—that was all a lie.
  But at the altar, tears and lamentations,
  the fateful preparations
  for my sacrifice—all these were true.

ORESTES: Dreadful, what our father dared to do.

IPHIGENIA: To be without a father was my fate.
But now we see
a change from old to new
created by the power of destiny.

ORESTES: What if you had actually
sacrificed me,
poor woman?

IPHIGENIA: How could I bear
to dare what I did dare?
You as the victim, I the executioner,
we came so close, we came so close, my brother,
to that unholy slaughter.
But what will happen next? Where will this go?
What fate, what destiny,
will confront me now?
How can I find a way to send you home,
far from this place,
this country where the custom is to kill,
and back to Argos, where you first came from,
before the sword, the sword that thirsts for blood,
gives chase?
This is my challenge now:
to discover how,
to puzzle out which way to get you home,
whether on dry land,
no ship, but step by step,
no roads, no path—
that way you walk near death.
But then by sea? The Blue
Black Rocks, the narrow strait—
a long and perilous voyage,
a desperate flight.
What should I do in this extremity?

What divinity,
what mortal man,
what creature in between
earth and heaven could find
a way? There is no way
for Atreus' poor children to be free,
to win release from this catastrophe.

CHORUS: This is a wonder well beyond the reach
of rumor, or of any human speech.
But having seen, not merely heard it, I
know that it is true.

PYLADES: Orestes, when dear friends encounter friends,
of course they will clasp one another's hands,
embrace, and weep. But no more lamentation!
Now we must assess the situation:
how to escape from this barbarian place
and turn instead toward safety's shining face
as toward the sun.
A careful man
must follow out his fate
and seize his chances—and they may be sweet.

ORESTES: You're right. And I think luck is on our side.
To those who strive with all their heart and mind,
the heavens are more likely to be kind.

IPHIGENIA: But first you cannot stop my asking you:
how is my sister—how's Electra? She
and her fate touch me.

ORESTES: This man here—Electra is his wife.
They live together. Theirs is a good life.

IPHIGENIA: What country does he come from, and whose son
is he?

ORESTES: Strophius the Phocian
　　is his father.

IPHIGENIA: 　　　Atreus' daughter, then,
　　was his mother? He and we are kin.

ORESTES: Our cousin, yes—and my only true friend.

IPHIGENIA: He wasn't born yet—now I understand—
　　when father sacrificed me.

ORESTES: 　　　　　　　No, not then.
　　Strophius remained childless for some time.

IPHIGENIA: Oh husband of my sister, I greet you.

ORESTES: Not only kinsman but my savior, too.

IPHIGENIA: But now I need to know:
　　that thing you did to Mother,
　　that dreadful thing—how, how could you do that?

ORESTES: Of that we will not speak.
　　What I did was done
　　to avenge our father.

IPHIGENIA: Our mother killed her husband, yes. I try
　　to understand: why did she do it? Why?

ORESTES: Your mother's reasons—it is not good for you
　　to hear them mentioned, let alone to know.

IPHIGENIA: I obey you. I am silent. So . . .
　　tell me: does Argos now
　　look to you to be its ruler?

ORESTES: No.
    The king is Menelaus there. And I—
    I am an exile and a refugee.

IPHIGENIA: Can it be
    our uncle has harmed our poor family,
    done violence to our sad ancestral house?

ORESTES: No, not our uncle. It was my fear
    of the Furies that
    hounded me out of there.

IPHIGENIA: The Furies chased and harried you, I know,
    to punish you according to their law
    for matricides—

ORESTES: Yes, they
    forced their bloody bit into my jaw.

IPHIGENIA: So that was what caused your delirium here.
    People saw you raving on the shore.

ORESTES: I have been seen before
    frenzied and foaming.

IPHIGENIA: But what brought you to this desolate land?

ORESTES: I came obedient to the god's command—
    Apollo's oracle.

IPHIGENIA: To do what task?
    Unless you're sworn to silence, may I ask?

ORESTES: I am allowed to tell you what it was
    that spelled the start of all my many woes.
    That business with our mother—let me say
    only that pollution came that way.

I was unclean. The Furies then gave chase,
harried me, raving, zigzag, place to place.
Finally Apollo put a stop to this
and ordered me to Athens to be tried
before those goddesses whose name is dread
to speak. There is a sacred
court there, dedicated
by Zeus when his son Ares was polluted
by murder. When I arrived in Athens first,
no one would receive me as a guest—
who would house a man the gods detest?
Even those who sheltered me required
that all alone I ate what they prepared.
In their own homes they kept me separate,
no one to speak to as I drank or ate.
Pouring in separate vessels, everyone
took private pleasure in his cup of wine.
For the Athenians my woe has become,
from what I understand, a ritual;
now drinkers never fill their pitchers full.

I came to the Hill of Ares to be tried.
I stood on one side;
the eldest Fury faced me on the other.
I heard the charge that I had killed my mother.
When I had answered it, Apollo saved
me with the evidence he had to give.
Athena counted out the votes; I won.
That dreadful trial over, I was gone.
Some Furies—those persuaded by my case—
chose the trial's precinct for their holy place.
But some believed that I was guilty; they
hounded me, pursued me tirelessly
until I came to Phoebus' shrine again.
And there before his temple I lay down
and swore I never would touch food; swore I
had singled out this holy place to die

unless the very god
whose machinery
had ruined me
so thoroughly
could somehow undo
the wreckage he had caused—could somehow be,
instead of my destruction, my salvation.
From Phoebus' golden tripod then I heard
a voice that spoke, and this is what it said:

"A statue of Artemis
has fallen from the air
into the Taurian land.
And this is my command
to you: go there
and seize the statue, then
return with it to Athens once again."

So, sister, now I doubly beg for help from you.
If I get my hands on this statue,
then I will finally obtain release,
relief from my madness.
Not only will my long delirium cease,
but when I take a ship and sail away
from this place to Mycenae,
I will bring you with me.
Oh dearest sister, save your family,
our ancestry, save me!
If I cannot obtain
this statue, then our life
will fall to utter ruin.

CHORUS: Some superhuman rage inflicts destruction
    on generation after generation.

IPHIGENIA: Oh my dear brother, long before you came,
    my greatest wish was always and only to be home

in Argos and to see you there.
What you desire is what I desire:
to untie the knot of your long pain
and set you free and get you home again.
Even if a father sacrificed his daughter—
let that go. To put our house in order
is my dearest wish. Rescuing you,
I save our race from further slaughter too—
I will not have to sacrifice you. But
my fear is this: the goddess will find out
what I have done—the goddess and the king.
The empty pedestal, the statue gone—
when they see
this, they will blame me.
How can I then escape execution?
What could my excuse be?
If we can see our way to doing this,
stealing the statue, taking me—then yes,
a glorious undertaking, worth the risk.
If we should stumble, then
even if you make your way back home,
my life is at an end.
But I am not afraid, so let us try,
Even if saving you means I must die.
A family trembles when a man is lost;
everyone knows a woman counts for less.

ORESTES: No!
I am my mother's murderer—and now
I cannot stain my hands with your blood too.
We have a single purpose, you and I—
a goal we share whether we live or die.
If I reach home, I will bring you with me;
if I die here, then I remain with you.

But listen; I have thought of something. Say
all that has happened is contrary to

the will of Artemis—if so, then why
should Loxias command
me to take Artemis' statue back
to Athens, to the goddess's native land?
Why would Apollo bring me to this place
first as a victim, then to see your face?
All these facts for me
add up to certainty
that we will make our way
home to safety—you,
my beloved sister, you and I.

IPHIGENIA: But how to win what both of us desire?
    The trouble with our journey home lies there.
    We do not lack the will; we lack a way.

ORESTES: What if we should slay
    the king?

IPHIGENIA: For foreigners to kill a king—
    dreadful to mention such a dangerous thing.

ORESTES: But we must risk it, if it saves our lives.

IPHIGENIA: I praise the boldness of such an enterprise,
    but as for me,
    I could never do it.

ORESTES: What if secretly
    you hid me in the temple here?

IPHIGENIA: So—yes;
    could we escape with nighttime cloaking us?

ORESTES: Thieves thrive in darkness; honesty loves the sun.

IPHIGENIA: But there are watchmen posted in this shrine,
and they will see us.

ORESTES: Oh, what can we do?
How can we even hope to get away?

IPHIGENIA: I think a new plan has occurred to me.

ORESTES: Tell me! Share it, so I know it too.

IPHIGENIA: My plan is: cleverly
to use your sufferings, your long agony.

ORESTES: Women are artful—they can find a way.

IPHIGENIA: Here is what I will say:
you've come from Argos as a matricide.

ORESTES: Use all my troubles, if this does us good.

IPHIGENIA: I'll say you can't be sacrificed, because—

ORESTES: —of what? I can guess what you're about to say:
I cannot be sacrificed, because—

IPHIGENIA: —your pollution violates our laws.
The offered victim must be pure.

ORESTES: But how
does this idea help us find a way
to seize the statue?

IPHIGENIA: To cleanse you in the sea—
that's what I'll ask permission to do.

ORESTES: But how does that idea help us take
the statue of Artemis for whose sake

I sailed here, and that still
stands within the temple?

IPHIGENIA: This is how it helps us: I will say
that since you touched the statue, you
polluted it, and I must cleanse it too.

ORESTES: To purify the statue—
I see. But where will you go?
Will you take it to some deserted bay,
rocky, remote—

IPHIGENIA: Where your ship lies
at anchor and its woven cables sway—
I will go that way.

ORESTES: Will you alone
carry the statue, or allow someone
else to touch it?

IPHIGENIA: I'll take it. Only I
may touch the image—no one else but me.

ORESTES: What part in all this will Pylades play,
my dear companion?

IPHIGENIA: I will simply say
he bears the same pollution as you do.

ORESTES: This plot you'll carry out—will the king know?
Or will it all be surreptitiously
managed?

IPHIGENIA: No, that cannot be.
I'll use my wiles to tell him, cleverly
persuading him. There is no means to hide

what we are up to. Meanwhile you must make sure
that everything is ready where you are.

ORESTES: My ship is ready and waiting. But we need
one more assurance: can these women hide
what we are planning? Can they be discreet?
Your task is to persuade them, to entreat
their silence. Women understand the spell
pity can cast. And then—all may go well.

IPHIGENIA: Women, dear women, I turn to you.
You are the ones with power now
to make this tale end happily
or crash into catastrophe,
the loss of all that's dear to me—
the loss of my country and my brother,
the loss of my beloved sister.
And let the first plea that I make
be for our common gender's sake.
We know that women help each other;
we know we're all in this together.
Be silent! Breathe no word about
our desperate effort to get out.
A noble thing is a loyal tongue.
We three friends here are bound by one
common fate that's plain to see:
eager to get back home or die
together. I promise, if I do
reach home, to share my luck with you:
I will bring you as well to Greece.
So, women, I implore you: please,
by your right hand, your cheeks, your knees,
by those at home whom you have lost,
by those at home you love the most—
mother, father, children—say:
Will you help us? Do you agree,

do you refuse? For if you do,
I'm dead—I and my brother too.

CHORUS: Courage, dear lady—only get away!
    Zeus be my witness, I will say
    nothing of all this. I will keep
    your secret safe.

IPHIGENIA: Oh, may you reap
    rewards for this,
    and happiness!
    And now I turn to you and you,
    and here is what you have to do.
    The king of this place will soon appear,
    the reason for his visit here
    to learn: Has the rite been carried out?
    Have the foreigners' throats been cut?
    Oh lady Artemis, you who saved my life
    in Aulis, when my father raised the knife,
    save me again!
    And save these two young men!
    If you fail to save
    our lives, then why should anyone believe
    Apollo's prophecies are ever true?
    This barbarous country is no place for you,
    Artemis! Leave it! Go to Athens! Why
    stay here when you can dwell
    in a city full
    of holiness, tranquillity, and joy?

[*Exit* IPHIGENIA, ORESTES, *and* PYLADES.]

CHORUS: Bird on the cliffs above the sea,
    your song is of catastrophe,
    and those who hear you can perceive
    it's for your husband that you grieve.
    Halcyon bird, I have no wings,

but I too am a bird that sings—
I can lament as well as you.
I long for the Greece that once I knew,
I long for Lady Artemis,
guardian of childbirth, kind goddess
who lives by the Hill of Cynthus, near
the date palm with its fronds like hair,
near the graceful laurel tree,
near the olive, green and gray,
sacred to Leto's girl and boy.
I long for the lake that swirls nearby,
whirlpool of waters, where the swan
honors the Muses with her song.
My cheeks are wet,
my tears run down,
they took me prisoner
when my town
fell in the war—
they brought me here
on shipboard, captive of the spear.
Then I was sold,
and so I came
to this strange barbarian home.
My task here is to wait upon
the daughter of Agamemnon.
She serves the goddess who slays deer—
sheep are never victims here.
I attend her at the altar,
holy place of ritual slaughter.

The man who has never had good luck—
I envy him! When he is struck
by a change of fortune from good to bad,
he does not miss what he never had.
Accustomed to hard necessity,
he is inured to misery.
But to have tasted peace and joy,

and then to lose them, seems to me
a heavy fate for mortals to bear,
a burden of endless misery.

My lady, that is not your lot.
As panpipe music marks the beat,
rowers will bend and strain and sweat
to speed you home in an Argive ship
with fifty oarsmen. Apollo too
will clasp his lyre and sing for you—
will hymn your safe arrival in
brilliant Athens. I cannot go,
lady; I cannot follow you.
You sail swiftly, sped by the wind
over the ocean; I'm left behind.
On that bright track if I could go
where the fires of Helios glow—
but no.

If I were in my own bedroom . . .
but my wings would slow if I were home,
my wings would stop. Instead, let me
dance, as my dancing used to be.
A virgin of good family,
beside my mother, I whirled and spun.
Of all the girls in my generation,
would I be the lucky one
to drape myself in luxury—
all those silky things to wear,
a rainbow veil to kiss my skin,
and my face shaded by my long hair—
was this a contest I could win?

[*Enter* THOAS.]

THOAS: The Greek woman who guards this temple's gate—
    where is she? Has she sacrificed them yet,

the strangers? Are they being burned within
the innermost sanctuary of the shrine?

[*Enter* IPHIGENIA, *carrying a statue.*]

CHORUS: She's here, my lord. She'll tell you the whole story
   clearly and truthfully.

THOAS: What is this I see?
   Daughter of Agamemnon, tell me why
   you've pried this statue from her sacred home
   and carry her like luggage in your arms?

IPHIGENIA: Stop in the threshold! Do not step within—

THOAS: The temple? Why? What deed can have been done?

IPHIGENIA [*spitting*]: Phtou, phtou!
   Let me avert
   any hurt.
   May holiness
   cleanse this place.

THOAS: What do you mean? What's happened? Make it clear!

IPHIGENIA: The sacrificial victims captured here—
   my lord, they were polluted.

THOAS: You know this?
   If so, from whom? Or is it a mere guess?

IPHIGENIA: The statue of the goddess turned away.

THOAS: All by itself? An earthquake, I surmise,
   or other natural possibilities—

IPHIGENIA: All by itself. And then it closed its eyes.

THOAS: What was the reason—that they were unclean?

IPHIGENIA: That reason is enough. What they have done
    is hideous, unspeakable.

THOAS: Did they
    kill a barbarian down by the sea?

IPHIGENIA: Their hands were stained with blood before they came
    to this temple—stained with blood from home.

THOAS: What blood? Whose blood? I want to know!

IPHIGENIA: Together
    they joined their swords and murdered their own mother.

THOAS: Lord Apollo! No barbarian
    would dare commit the act these two have done.

IPHIGENIA: Yes—a crime so vile
    all Greece declared their sentence was exile.

THOAS: So this is why you bring the statue here?

IPHIGENIA: Yes—out in the open, where the heavens may clear
    the taint of blood.

THOAS: These foreigners' pollution—
    how did you obtain this information?

IPHIGENIA: Easily. When the goddess turned away,
    I questioned them.

THOAS: Greece raised a gem in you—
    so careful and so clever and so wise.

IPHIGENIA: And they told me, to set my mind at ease—

THOAS: Good news from Argos would work like a charm.

IPHIGENIA: —they said Orestes had escaped all harm,
that he was doing well, my only brother.

THOAS: So joy would make you change the doom of slaughter.

IPHIGENIA: That wasn't all the news they had to tell.
They said my father was alive and well.

THOAS: And how did you respond? It seems to me
the goddess here still claims your loyalty.

IPHIGENIA: Of course. I hate Greece. Greece has ruined me.

THOAS: About these strangers—tell me what to do.

IPHIGENIA: We must be guided now
by custom, ancient precedent, and law.

THOAS: Then why do I not see you wield a sword?
Where is the basin that should catch the blood?

IPHIGENIA: First I must cleanse the strangers of pollution
by washing them.

THOAS: At a spring? Or in the ocean?

IPHIGENIA: In the sea,
which rinses every human stain away.

THOAS: I understand—such victims would be purer.

IPHIGENIA: And my own situation would be better.

THOAS: Right here the waves break—on this holy space.

IPHIGENIA: For what I plan, a more deserted place
would be better.

THOAS: Go where you need to go;
I will not witness what I must not see.

IPHIGENIA: And there is one more thing I need to do:
this image here must be purified too.

THOAS: Yes, if it bears the stain of matricide.

IPHIGENIA: That is why I took it from inside.

THOAS: You perform rituals with such thought and care,
no wonder everyone admires you here.

IPHIGENIA: Now this is what I need.

THOAS: Speak and it's yours.

IPHIGENIA: Please put shackles on these foreigners.

THOAS: But even if they broke free, there is no place
they could escape to.

IPHIGENIA: I do not trust Greece
or any Greeks.

THOAS: Bring out the shackles, you attendants there.

IPHIGENIA: And let them also lead the victims here—

THOAS: It will be done—

IPHIGENIA: —with heads and faces covered.

THOAS: Yes, to shield the sun
　　from their pollution.

IPHIGENIA: Some of your servants should accompany me.

THOAS: These people here will go along with you.

IPHIGENIA: And one last thing.
　　Send someone to the city to proclaim—

THOAS: What?

IPHIGENIA: Let all the citizens obey:
　　to go inside their houses and to stay
　　there.

THOAS:　　Yes—to keep clear
　　of pollution, of old bloodshed?

IPHIGENIA: Precisely. Such stains spread.

THOAS: You, there—go, announce this to the city—

IPHIGENIA: —that no one should approach. No one should see.

THOAS: You protect our city lovingly.

IPHIGENIA: Yes—and those who are most dear to me.

THOAS: It must be me you are referring to.

IPHIGENIA: Yes—and now this is what I need from you.
　　Stay here before the temple.

THOAS:　　　　　　　　　　　What shall I do?

IPHIGENIA: Take this torch: purify
the sanctuary
with fire.

THOAS: It will be clean,
pristine, when you return.

IPHIGENIA: And when the foreign victims come outside—

THOAS: What should I do?

IPHIGENIA: —cover your eyes. Your head
should be wrapped in your cloak.

THOAS: So I won't see
these bloodstained criminals as they pass by.

IPHIGENIA: But if it seems to you that I delay,
that I am gone too long—

THOAS: How can I know
how long you should be gone?

IPHIGENIA: —you must stay calm.

THOAS: Perform the needed rituals; take your time.

IPHIGENIA: Oh, may
these purifying rites succeed, I pray!

THOAS: And I pray too,
lady. I pray for the same thing as you.

[*Enter* ORESTES *and* PYLADES, *heads covered.*]

IPHIGENIA: I see the strangers moving into the light of day.
I see the goddess's festive finery.

I see the newborn lambs whose blameless blood will wash away
stale bloodstains. And I see the blazing torches glow.
Everything is in place to purify
these foreigners, and cleanse the goddess too.

To the townspeople gathered here I now have this to say:
fear this miasma and keep far away.
Whether you are a guardian of the temple here
whose hands must be kept reverent and pure,
or whether to be married is your plan,
or you will give birth soon,
keep away!
Pollution can move swiftly; you must fly.

O maiden goddess Artemis, O Zeus and Leto's daughter,
if I wash away the foulness of this ancient murder,
if I perform the needed sacrifice here at the altar,
the temple that you dwell in will be pure,
fortune will smile on us. I say no more;
but send my thoughts unspoken to the gods above, who know,
and most of all, my lady Artemis, to you.

[*Exit* IPHIGENIA, ORESTES, *and* PYLADES.]

CHORUS: In the fertile valley of Delos isle,
     Leto gave birth to her beautiful
     son—god Apollo, with golden hair,
     a skilled performer on the lyre
     and archer whose arrows never fail.
     From a cliff beside the sea
     she spirited her son away—
     away from the place whose lasting fame
     was to have been where the god was born;
     up to Parnassus' lofty peak
     where Dionysian dancers leap
     and torrents tumble over rocks
     she brought him. But a monstrous snake,

gigantic, with a face as black
as wine, and patterns on its back,
a dreadful dragon, born of earth,
haunted the sacred laurel grove,
sliding its coils around each tree
in the holy precinct of Delphi.

You were still an infant then,
bouncing on your mother's arm,
Apollo, but you brought it down!
You killed the python and took your seat
at the oracle's holy heart.
On a golden tripod now you sit
and from your throne of truth give out
to mortal men who need to know
decrees derived from sacred law.
Your innermost sanctuary lies
where the stream of Castalia flows;
the shrine where you preside was built
in the middle of the world.
But after Apollo took away
from Themis, daughter of the Earth,
Themis, goddess of righteousness,
her place at the seat of prophecy,
then Earth sent in retaliation
a nightly brood of dreams and visions
which showed the mass of humanity
what had been and what would be.
Jealous for the honor
of her daughter,
Earth used this ploy
to take away
Apollo's power of prophecy.
Up to Olympus the god sped then
and wound his arm around Zeus's throne,
begging his father to liberate

the Pythian temple from Earth's hate.
Zeus laughed that his son, while still a child,
should show such early lust for gold,
for worship that would bring him wealth,
all of it stolen by the Earth.
Zeus tossed his head and put an end
to the voices that spoke to mortal men,
telling the truth all through the night,
and gave this honor back again
to Apollo, his own son,
who now, seated on his throne,
chants to the visitors who crowd in
from far and near
so they can hear
the god-given
decrees of heaven
from divine lips to their ears.

[*Enter* MESSENGER.]

MESSENGER: Temple attendants, and you men who guard
    the altar, King Thoas has disappeared.
    Where can he have gone?
    Pry the great doors open.
    Is he in there,
    inside the temple? Let him come out here.

CHORUS: May I ask what is the matter?

MESSENGER: The matter is Agamemnon's clever daughter.
    She plotted for the two young foreigners
    to flee our shores
    and take with them
    the stolen image of our Artemis—
    so our dear goddess
    now lies in a ship that's bound for Greece.

CHORUS: Incredible, the tale you tell! But he,
the king you wish to see,
has rushed out of the temple and is gone.

MESSENGER: Where? He should hear all that's been going on.

CHORUS: Where I do not know. You go seek him out
and find him—then deliver your report.

MESSENGER: What a mistake, to trust a woman! You
helped her out
with this conspiracy, I do not doubt.

CHORUS: You're raving. Two doomed foreigners run away—
what difference does that make to me?
Now you run to the gate—
go find your master there.

MESSENGER: No, I will not, till someone makes it clear
whether the king is inside or not.
Open the gate,
tell your master I am standing here
at the door
with my delivery:
an ample cargo of catastrophe.

THOAS: Who is this
knocking so loudly, the entire house
reverberates with noise?

MESSENGER: These women tried
to tell me that you were not here—they lied.
You were inside here, hiding, all this time.

[*Enter* THOAS.]

THOAS: What was their motive in these lies to you?

MESSENGER: That can wait. But here's what you must do
        and do without delay.
    The young woman who tended
    the altar in this place,
    Iphigenia—she has run away
    with the two foreigners; and she has taken
    the image of our goddess Artemis
    away from us.
    All that confabulation
    about purification
    was a clever ruse.

THOAS: What are you saying? You astonish me.
    What could possibly be
    the inspiration
    for an act that boggles my imagination?

MESSENGER: There's more to tell. Wait: this beggars belief.
    Her motive was to save Orestes' life.

THOAS: Orestes who? The son
    born to Tyndareus' daughter—
    is that the man you mean?

MESSENGER: That's the one.
    Clytemnestra's son—
    Orestes is his name—
    that is the same
    man she dedicated
    to our goddess at the altar.

THOAS: I am bewildered. I—
    what else can I say?

MESSENGER: Listen to me,
    my king. You must not turn your mind that way.
    Your thoughts now must not stray

from the task at hand.
Think! Be strategic! Plan
a method of pursuit.
Your goal must be to catch these fugitives;
first you must hunt them out.

THOAS: Of course you are right.
So keep advising me—
say more. Theirs is no short
journey as they flee,
and I, the king, have troops at my command.
They can't escape my land.

MESSENGER: Let me tell you how it happened. When
we came down to the shore,
and Orestes' ship was anchored there
in secret, we who'd been
commanded to bring shackles for these men,
these foreigners, by Agamemnon's daughter—
well, she gave us another order then:
to keep our distance from the sacred flame,
to stand aside and so avoid pollution
of the purification,
of the consecration,
of the ceremony
she planned there. Meanwhile, she
paced behind the foreigners, their shackles in her hands—
a strange proceeding, hard to understand,
suspicious—but the guards whom you had sent,
uncertain what it meant,
agreed to it.

Time passed. And meanwhile she—
so we would trust in her activity—
chanted and wailed in a barbarian mode
as if to cleanse the stain of stale spilt blood.
We sat there waiting. Then we wondered whether

the strangers could have freed themselves together
and killed our mistress and escaped from there.
Why did we sit in silence, then? For fear
of seeing what we were forbidden to.
Finally we all agreed what we must do:
we had to go, although it was forbidden,
to where we thought the strangers might be hidden.

And there we saw it—a Greek ship,
oars at the ready, poised like wings,
fifty sailors ready to row,
to bend their oars and fly away—
and there were the two young men, now free.
They stood on deck looking out to sea.
The crew was busy everywhere—
some at the prow, some at the anchor,
while others hurried with a ladder
and let it down into the sea
so the foreign girl could get away.
But having seen
her tricks and schemes,
her plots and all her clever lies,
we could not let her simply fly.
Grasping the tiller that steered the ship
by its roots we tugged it out.
Now angry words flew through the air.
We shouted at them: "How do you dare
to steal our holy images,
abduct their guardian priestesses
out of our country, whoever you are?
What is your name? Who was your sire
that you take this woman away from here?"
He said to us: "Orestes is my name.
Know that I am Agamemnon's son
and this woman's brother—she who was
lost to our family, taken from us.
I have come here to bring her back home."

He spoke, but we would not give up the fight;
we still held tight
to the foreign woman,
trying to force her to
come along with us, my king, to you.
That is why my cheeks—
you see?—are bruised and bleeding. We
had no weapons in our hands
and neither did the Greeks,
but they—those two young men—
pummeled us so violently,
liver, lungs, our bodies everywhere,
all our limbs trembled. We were in agony.
Bearing the marks of these vicious attacks,
we fled up toward the rocks—
heads, faces, eyes all torn and bloody. We
found a hilltop; from there
we kept attacking, but more cautiously.
We pelted them with stones,
but archers on the ship kept us away
with their drawn bows,
with arrows. Finally
we were defeated, and we had to flee.
A giant wave now washed the ship toward shore.
But in her fear
the virgin would not set her foot on land.
So Orestes, her brother,
hoisted her onto his left shoulder,
waded into the water,
and jumped onto the ladder;
thus stowing on board not only his sister
but what he grasped tight in his other hand:
that statue fallen from heaven,
the image of Zeus's daughter Artemis.
And from within the ship a voice
cried out, "Oh men of Greece,
sailors, bend to your oars,

beat the blue water into creamy foam
and sail, sail, sail towards home.
We came for this
through the Symplegades
to the Unfriendly, the
Inhospitable Sea—
we have our prize, now let us sail away!"

At this, a sweet shout rose from every
throat as the sailors headed out to sea.
While still within the harbor,
the ship moved easily;
but once it had emerged to open water
and was about to sail,
a fearful gale
suddenly struck
and pushed it back and back
to shore. The sailors struggled,
kicking at the wave, but hopelessly—
the ship was being borne back from the open sea
and toward land.
Agamemnon's child now took a stand
and prayed aloud: "Oh Leto's daughter,
Lady Artemis,
bring me, your priestess,
safely back to Greece
from this godforsaken
place! As for the image I have taken—
goddess, pardon me!
You love your brother; I
love my brother too.
It was this love that made me do
what I had to do."

Then all the sailors sang aloud
a paean to the god,
and each, his strong arms bare,

bent to his oar
at the boatswain's command.
But more and more the ship
seemed about to strike
the rocks, where it would wreck.
One of our men now stepped into the sea;
another handily
readied a rope to fasten to the ship.
As for me,
they sent me here to you, my king.
My mission: to report on everything.

My advice now to you:
take the shackles in your hands,
seize the ropes, and go.
Unless the swell subsides, unless the sea
somehow grows calm again, there is no way,
there is no hope,
for the fugitives; they cannot escape.
Lord Poseidon watches over Troy;
Greeks have always been his enemy.
He hates Pelops' descendants especially.
So you see
he gives you now this opportunity
at one and the same time
to seize Orestes, Agamemnon's son,
and his sister Iphigenia—she
who has forgotten she was sacrificed
to the goddess Artemis,
to the goddess whose priestess she was,
to the goddess whom she now betrays.

CHORUS: Iphigenia, my heart bleeds for you,
    miserable lady, once again to be
    delivered to the king, your enemy,
    with your brother, and condemned to die!

THOAS: Listen, every citizen,
    all you men of this barbarian land:
    saddle your horses, gallop to the shore,
    and gather up the wreck
    of the Greek ship.
    Then, with the goddess helping, hunt them down
    swiftly, these godless, these blasphemous men.
    Do not delay!
    And you, you others, drag the ships down to the beach.
    Either on the water or dry land,
    these foreigners are not beyond our reach.
    We'll gallop after them and run them down
    and then we'll either hurl them from the rocks
    or skewer them with stakes
    piercing their bodies.

    And I know you all,
    you women, had a role
    in this conspiracy.
    When I am at leisure, you will pay.
    But I cannot be idle now.
    I have more important work to do.

[*Enter aloft* ATHENA.]

ATHENA: King Thoas, wait!
    Where are you off to in such hot pursuit?
    I am the goddess Athena.
    Listen to me.
    Abandon the chase. Stop this fiercely flowing
    torrent of soldiers which you have set going
    and which is now about to flood the land.
    Apollo's oracle and not mere chance
    has knotted this thick web of circumstance.
    Orestes was hounded
    for years and years
    from city to city

all over Greece
trying to flee
the Furies' rage—
who but Apollo brought him here?
Weary, forever on the run,
Orestes tried at the same time
to save his sister stranded here—
to carry Iphigenia home to Argos—
and also bring the image of the goddess
and deliver it to me
in holy Athens, my dear city,
and so to end his misery.
This much I have to say to you.
And this: you are deluded if you plan
to seize this man
out on the stormy ocean.
Poseidon, who commands the sea,
as a favor to me
is already soothing, already smoothing
the broad backs of the waves, creating still
waters that the ship may cross at will.
Orestes, here are my
instructions for you—
you hear my voice though you are far away—
take the statue, take your sister, and
depart from Taurus! Leave all this behind
and go where your fate calls,
to shining Athens—a god built its walls.
At the border of Attica
is a district called Carystia—
holy, and Halae is its name.
You must construct a temple there, to be
the final stop, the sacred space
where you will reverently place
the image you have carried, carried far.
And name it for the Taurian land
which you escaped and left behind.

Commemorate your trials as you
were whipped and hounded to and fro,
from pillar to post,
from city to city
all over Greece—the Furies have no pity.
And future festivals will celebrate:
will sing hymns to commemorate
both your story and the goddess
Artemis—Taurian Artemis.
This too you must lay down as law:
On the feast day every year
let a sword be held to a man's neck;
let the blade graze it; let it nick
the flesh enough for blood to run.
With this act you will atone
for your interrupted sacrifice
to the goddess Artemis—
both honor her and satisfy
the demands of piety.

Your task, Iphigenia,
is this: you will become
Artemis' guardian priestess
in her new holy home,
the temple at Brauron.
And in that temple, when you die,
they will bury you.
To you they'll dedicate
the beautiful, elaborate woven dresses
which women who die in childbirth
leave behind them in their widowed houses.

As for these Greek women here,
women who have been your faithful friends,
my mission is to lead them
from this strange land back home.

Orestes, I have saved you once before,
in my own Athens, when you were being tried.
I can save you once more.
And ever after, when a jury's vote is tied,
let the defendant win.
This shall be the custom from now on.
So, son of Agamemnon,
take your sister; leave this place forever.
And you, King Thoas, may you not feel anger.

THOAS: Lady Athena, whoever would dispute
a god's commands cannot be thinking right.
Against Orestes here
I feel no rancor
for taking the statue away;
nor do I feel anger at his sister.
This is the gods' decree.
Safe voyage and calm waters and success
in transporting the image of the goddess
to her new resting place—
may all these go with you!
I will reverse my orders,
cancel the spears,
halt the oars,
let your ship sail in peace across the ocean.
All the resistance that I set in motion
I will undo,
goddess, since my orders came from you.

ATHENA: Congratulations! What must be must be.
Fate has power over both you and me.
And yes, let favorable winds now blow
for Agamemnon's son,
sending him safely to
Athens. I will go
along with him—divinity unsleeping,
his sister and the statue in my keeping.

Prosperous voyage—go
in blessedness. *Sto kalo!*

CHORUS: Blessed among mortals and immortals too,
    Athena, we shall do
    all you command us to!
    The words I hear from you
    bring unexpected joy,
    they make my heart leap high
    with triumph and delight,
    oh lady Victory.
    May you desert me never,
    may you be my guardian forever!

This manuscript could not have been prepared for publication without the expert and timely help—under pressure—of Bryanna Tidmarsh, my student, assistant, and friend, and a person of remarkable energy and focus. Thank you, Bryanna.